NOT JUST ANOTHER EMBROIDERY BOOK

Lark Books
50 College Street
Asheville, North Carolina 28801

Printed in Hong Kong by South China Printing Company

10 9 8 7 6 5 4 3 2 1

Library of Congress Cataloging-in-Publication Data:

Not just another embroidery book.

   Bibliography: p.
   Includes index.
   1. Embroidery—Patterns. I. Stiles, Phyllis,
1956-
TT771.N68   1986   746.44   86-7140
ISBN 0-937274-23-2 (pbk.)

NOT JUST ANOTHER EMBROIDERY BOOK

Edited by Phyllis Stiles

Lark Books
Asheville, North Carolina

CONTENTS

INTRODUCTION

Of all the types of embroidery, free-style is the most popular by far. As its name implies, it is much less restrictive than most embroidery forms. This book is devoted exclusively to free-style embroidery.

Why is it so loved by the thread artist? First of all, it borrows stitches from other styles and adds to them its own wealth of stitches. There is such a variety of stitches that most sources divide them into families, such as outline, filling, and looped stitches. In the outline family alone, you could choose from ten different stitches for producing a line, be it an outline, a design line, or a border.

Another reason for its popularity is that free-style embroidery can be worked on almost any fabric and with almost any thread, so long as the two work well together. Other embroidery forms, such as cross stitch and needlepoint, require thread counting, hence must be worked on even-weave or canvas fabrics. The expense of special fabrics and the tedium of counting threads cause many people to shy away from counted thread work. But in free-style embroidery, if you can transfer a design to a fabric, either directly, or indirectly by means of waste canvas or an equivalent, you can embroider that design. One of the projects in this book is made of grass cloth which is embroidered with raffia!

In short, free-style embroidery entices you to be creative. Consequently, in this book we try to appeal to your spirit of adventure by presenting projects that use embroidery in offbeat places and which specify unusual materials and techniques. But please don't use our designs only as we have shown them. Add to them, combine them, change the colors—let them be inspiration for your own original free-style embroidery!

THE EMBROIDERER'S TOOLS

NEEDLES

The choice of a needle becomes very simple once you begin to sew. How does it feel? The needle should draw the thread through the fabric without pulling the fabric out of shape or poking holes in it. Embroidery needles have longer eyes than ordinary sewing needles to accommodate the larger threads used. They are available in various sizes and are numbered according to size: the higher the number, the finer the needles. Three kinds of needles are commonly used for embroidery: crewel, chenille, and tapestry.

Crewel needles

Crewel needles are sharp needles with long eyes, and are available in sizes 1 through 10. They are used for fine and medium-weight embroidery, but not for canvas work. As a general rule, a size 7 needle is suitable for 2 to 3 strands of thread, and size 6 is suitable for 4 or more strands.

Chenille needles

These are short needles with eyes large enough to accommodate yarn. They are available in sizes 13 through 26, and are used with heavier threads and fabrics.

Tapestry needles

Tapestry needles have blunt points and large eyes, and are available in sizes 13 through 26. They are used on fabrics whose threads would be easily split by a sharp needle. A tapestry needle is a good choice for embroidering on knits.

THREAD SELECTION

Any filament could be used for embroidery thread. You could use telephone wire as thread, provided you could locate an implement to act as a needle and then maneuver the threaded needle in and out of a suitable fabric. In other words, be open-minded about thread choice, but be practical, too.

Your choice of thread should be based on the project's function. Will it be exposed to light or weather? Will it be laundered? Will it have to withstand heavy wear? If you're not absolutely sure which thread is appropriate, work up a sample. Notice whether the thread, fabric, and stitches work together. Wool threads might be perfect for loosely woven canvas, but impossible to pull through cotton lawn. On a wool sweater you might try wool thread or a pearl cotton depending on the weight of the knit. Also consider contrast. Matte cotton thread looks stunning on a satiny fabric, and silk threads and lustrous cotton threads bring a flat, tightly woven wool to life. Your embroidery should be seen. It might be subtle, as in whitework embroidery, but nonetheless should be visible. Note the threads used for the organdy collar on page 128.

When you buy more than one skein of a color in any thread, it is best to select skeins of the same dye lot as shades vary from lot to lot. The threads used for the projects in this book are Floss, Pearl Cotton, Brilliant Embroidery and Cutwork Thread, and Matte Cotton. We have specified DMC threads because they are reliable and usually available wherever embroidery supplies are sold. Of course, there are many other brands of thread from which to choose. A brief explanation of each follows.

Floss

Floss is the most common embroidery thread. It is a loosely twisted, six-stranded cotton that can be used as one thread, or divided into any number of strands appropriate to the fabric being embroidered It is generally colorfast, pre-shrunk, and available in a wide range of colors. Skeins come in lengths of 26 to 27 feet (8 - 8½ m). To avoid wasted time and the frustration of tangled floss, handle each skein with care. Tug the loose thread end carefully; if it slides right out from the wrapper, you chose the correct end. If it doesn't, locate the other loose end and tug at it. Unwind the skein and cut it into convenient lengths of about 20 inches (51cm). Braid or wind the lengths and fasten them together with a twist tie for easy access later. When you're ready to embroider, divide the lengths into strands by holding some strands between your lips, the others in one hand, and the undivided length in the remaining hand. Separating the lengths in this manner untwists the threads, which is advantageous for two reasons: the untwisted thread will make sewing smoother, and it will cover the fabric better. Also, if you do not plan to use all six strands, you must separate them. Unlike many other threads, floss has no nap and can be sewn from either direction without resistance.

Pearl cotton

More lustrous than floss, pearl cotton is a twisted, 2-ply thread which cannot be divided. It is available in sizes 3, 5, 8, and 12 (the smaller the number, the larger the diameter). Size 5 is the most versatile. It can be bought in skeins or balls.

Brilliant Embroidery and Cutwork Thread (Coton a broder)

This thread is excellent for embroidered edges. It is a slightly twisted cotton which cannot be divided. It is available in three sizes and in a limited range of colors.

Matte cotton

This is a very soft thread, both in texture and color, and is guaranteed not to shine. It is a fairly thick, tightly twisted 5-ply thread, used as a single thread on heavier fabrics. It is available in 10-yard (9m) skeins in a wide range of colors.

EMBROIDERY HOOPS

An embroidery hoop holds the fabric taut while you work. Use of a hoop is essential for maintaining even stitch tension which keeps the embroidery from puckering. With smaller designs, a hoop also makes the work area more accessible.

The circular or oval hoop is available in wood or plastic. It consists of two rings, one fitting inside the other. The outer ring has an opening that can be tightened or loosened by means of a screw.

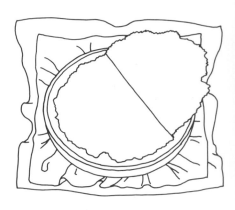

To mount the fabric in a hoop, first place the fabric, design side up, over the inner ring, then press the outer ring down around the inner ring. Adjust the fabric so it is smooth and taut, then adjust the screw tension to make the unit secure. Do not pull at the fabric once the hoop is tightened or it may become distorted. To protect existing embroidery as you move the hoop to make new areas accessible, place tissue paper over fabric before positioning the outer ring. Then, tear away paper from center of hoop.

If the fabric is too small to fit the hoop, simply baste it to a larger piece of fabric and cut away the added fabric from behind the area to be embroidered. Then mount the fabric as instructed above.

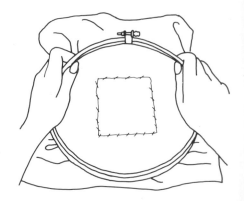

If the hoop is warped, or will not tighten up sufficiently, or you're afraid the screw will rust on the fabric, or if the fabric is

extremely delicate, wrap the outer ring in cotton bias tape
before placing it over the inner ring.

An embroidery stand is a handy device which attaches to the
hoop and frees the embroiderer's hands for sewing.

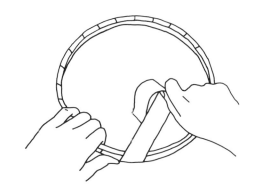

SCISSORS

Embroidery scissors are small, and have straight, pointed
blades. They should be used only to cut thread, either from
the skein or from the needle. Keep the points in a cork when
scissors are not in use.

A small pair of scissors with curved blades is very useful for
trimming fabric away from edges. They are a must for
precision cutting, such as trimming scalloped edges worked in
buttonhole stitch.

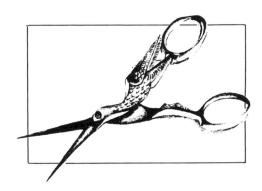

Scissors with long, straight blades are indispensable for cutting
fabric, and should be reserved for just that.

Always use the appropriate scissors for the job at hand. Using
the wrong scissors can inflict permanent damage upon work
that represents hours and hours of effort.

FOUNDATIONS FOR EMBROIDERING ON STRETCHY FABRICS

How do you transfer a design to a sweater? Easy! You
transfer the design to a piece of foundation material,
which is basted to the sweater and removed after
embroidering. The foundation can be waste canvas, etamine,
Trace Erase™, or ordinary tissue paper.

Waste canvas

Used mainly for needlework, this canvas is sold in a variety of
thread counts. Often it has printed blue lines to help in counted

thread embroidery such as cross stitch. It is a lifesaver for eyes that cannot stand the strain of counting threads. When the work is done, just pull the threads out one at a time. It enables you to achieve the look of counted thread work without the counting. It also works well as a foundation for embroidering on knits. It is commonly available where craft supplies are sold.

Etamine

This even-weave cotton/polyester blend is used for making pulled thread napkins and tablecloths. The looseness of the weave that enables you to pull threads is the quality which makes it ideal as a foundation for embroidering knits. It is softer than waste canvas, and therefore is more practical for backing embroidery on knits. It is not commonly sold in craft supply shops and it is expensive.

Trace Erase™

Erica Wilson's Trace Erase™ is similar to non-woven interfacing but not intended to be as durable. It is available with or without a printed grid. Embroider over it, and when the embroidery is complete tear it away with the help of tweezers. If some fabric remains under the embroidery, it will probably come out when the item is washed.

Tissue paper

Sometimes even tissue can be used as a backing and then be removed when embroidery is finished. It will not hold up as well as the other materials mentioned, however, so should not be used in projects requiring a long time for completion.

EMBROIDERY BASICS

TRANSFERRING DESIGNS

Thank goodness for modern technology. A hundred years ago, instructions for transferring a design might have read like this:

> The design is reproduced on tracing paper. The tracing paper is then laid upon a thickly folded cloth and pricked with a special needle. When the pricking is finished, the wrong side of the paper is rubbed with emery paper to remove the rough edges around the little holes. Afterward the pricked paper and fabric are secured with silk pins. A pouncing pad is prepared: a base covered in cloth is dipped in pounce powder, light for dark-colored fabrics and dark for light-colored fabrics. The surface of the pricked paper is rubbed with the pouncing pad. When the pouncing is finished, the design is traced. The paper is removed, any excess powder which might have passed through the holes is blown away, and the lines of the design are painted with a watercolor paint and a small sable brush.

This is a condensed version!

Today, transferring a design is slightly more time-efficient. There are some cases, however, where the pouncing method is still the best choice. Velvets, for example, are such temperamental fabrics that pouncing is the most effective way to transfer designs to them, as the nap precludes pressing with hot transfers and tracing with dressmaker's carbon. For most fabrics one or more of the following methods will be suitable. Of course, any method you choose should first be tested on a scrap. The last thing you want is a design that was not completely covered by embroidery and that will not wash out!

Commercial hot transfer designs

There is a great variety of pre-printed embroidery designs available. They are printed on paper with special transfer ink. When the paper is placed on fabric and pressed with a fairly hot iron, the ink is released onto the fabric. This is the simplest transfer method, but also the most risky in that the ink is intended to be permanent. Carefully consider the design and its placement before you begin. Take care not to move paper or fabric while you press, or the design will smudge. Pick up a corner when you begin pressing to be sure the design is taking; you may need to increase the iron's temperature. If the paper sticks to the fabric, run the iron over the paper again and gradually peel the paper away. To press, lift and lower the iron; don't slide it across the design or it will probably smudge.

Homemade hot transfers

Your own designs or designs from this book can be transferred to fabric by duplicating the commercial hot transfer process. Use a transfer pencil, available in craft, quilting, and embroidery supply stores, and transfer the design in reverse onto tissue paper. With the design side down, place the paper on fabric and press the paper lightly with a hot iron. Note the precautions given above for applying commercial hot transfers.

Carbon copies

Trace or draw the design onto fairly transparent paper. Cut a piece of carbon, either dressmaker's or ordinary typing carbon, just large enough to accommodate the design. You want to allow as little opportunity for smudging as possible. Pin the paper to the fabric and slip carbon in between, with carbon side toward fabric. Go over the design lines with a blunt tip, such as a small crochet hook or the head of a pin. A tracing wheel will work if the design isn't too intricate. The advantage of this method over the hot transfer method is that the designs can be washed out. Naturally, with the variety of carbon and fabrics available, you should make a test on a scrap first to be sure the carbon will wash out.

The magic window

If the fabric to be embroidered is fairly thin, you can draw or trace the design on tracing paper with a felt-tip pen, then hold or tape the paper and fabric against a sunlit window and trace the design onto the fabric with a soft lead pencil.

Pencil and paper

This method is widely practiced in countries where modern technology is scarce. For multiple tracings, such as scalloped edges, it is very effective; however, it works only on light-colored fabrics. Draw or trace the design on one side of a sheet of paper with a soft lead pencil. Then turn the sheet of paper over and trace the design from the opposite side. A sunlit window will make the job easier. Cover the lines of the design well by going over them repeatedly with the pencil. Place the heavily penciled side against the fabric and trace over the lines again with pencil. The soft lead will rub off onto the fabric. Flip the paper and trace the lines again. Each time you trace, you are replacing the lead that was rubbed off during the previous tracing, but you are also destroying the fragile paper. Hence, when the paper wears out, you must begin again.

Temporary foundations

Some fabrics, such as stretch knits, do not take transfers well. With these fabrics, the design is instead transferred to a foundation, the foundation basted to the fabric to be embroidered, and the embroidery worked through both layers. The foundation is then removed. See "Foundations for Embroidering on Stretchy Fabrics" on page 5 for complete instructions and suggested foundation materials.

FINISHING YOUR EMBROIDERY

Finishing is the best part of a project! Before you decide upon the most suitable methods for finishing your embroidery, be sure you understand the characteristics of the materials you've used. Take care in choosing your finishing methods; improper treatment of your piece at this stage can ruin your beautiful work.

Washing and cleaning

Your project might have taken months to complete, and by the time it's finished you may wonder whether there really is embroidery under all the dirt! Laundering or dry cleaning will bring your work back to life.

If you've used washable fabric and cotton thread or floss, your finished piece should be washable. Embroidery worked with silk thread usually must be dry cleaned. Use a good spot remover, or send it to a reputable dry cleaner.

If you used colored thread for your project, first check threads for colorfastness. Moisten a cotton ball with hot water and carefully pat the embroidery with it. If any color comes off on the cotton, the piece probably should be dry cleaned. Otherwise, wash the piece by hand in lukewarm water with mild soap. Squeeze it gently in the water; rubbing embroidery can damage the threads. Rinse first in lukewarm water, then in cold water, until the water runs clear. Roll the piece in a clean towel and pat gently to remove excess water. Hang it to dry, away from direct sunlight.

White-on-white embroidery should be washed by hand in hot water with a good liquid detergent. Squeeze it gently in the soapwater, then rinse in cold running water. Allow the piece to air dry in sunlight.

Pressing

Pressing not only removes wrinkles from the finished embroidery, but also can straighten fabric distortions resulting from uneven stitch tension. Before you press the piece, pad the ironing board well with a layer or two of towels. Place the embroidery, face down, on the padding and cover it with a pressing cloth. Use a dry cloth for a damp article, a damp cloth for a dry one. Set the iron at a temperature appropriate to the embroidered fabric. Press over the embroidered area very lightly, allowing the iron only to touch the cloth, not to weight it down. Too much pressure from the iron can flatten the embroidery.

Blocking

With free-style embroidery—the kind used for the projects in this book—proper washing and pressing usually will correct any distortion of the fabric caused by uneven stitch tension. If your particular project seems to require blocking, please refer to one of the good general embroidery books (several are listed at the back of this book) for a description of blocking techniques.

EMBROIDERY STITCHES

The stitches included in this section are only a sampling of those available to the free-style embroiderer. These were selected either because they are specified in the project instructions in this book, or simply because they are beautiful stitches that can be substituted for many of those mentioned in the instructions. Many spectacular pieces of embroidery have been entirely worked with just a single stitch!

Before you even thread your needle, please read the hints that follow. They could save you immeasurable time and frustration.

Hint 1.

Do not use knots. Begin the first thread by leaving a "tail" on the wrong side. As you embroider, catch the tail into the stitching for about two inches. To start the next new thread, slide thread through a row of stitches on the wrong side near the spot to be embroidered. Or, if you are pioneering a new area, follow the instructions above for beginning the first thread. To end a thread, pull it through to the wrong side and slip the needle through a row of stitches to a length of about two inches, then clip off the remainder.

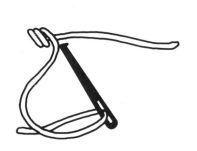 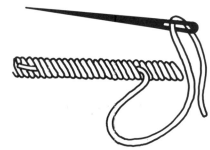 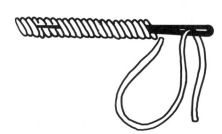

Hint 2.

Never carry a thread for a long distance on the wrong side. For distances of more than three-fourths inch (2cm), finish off threads as instructed above.

Hint 3.

If your thread gets twisted and tangled during stitching, simply allow needle to dangle for a few seconds until the thread unwinds.

Hint 4.

Completely cover all the design transfer markings with embroidery. Always insert the needle just outside the lines.

Hint 5.

To create realism in your design, first work those sections which will appear in relief, then the parts to appear raised.

ALGERIAN EYE STITCH

This stitch is traditionally a canvas embroidery stitch; yet it adapts very well to free-style embroidery and produces a lovely eyelet effect. For fabrics which are not evenly woven, or whose weave is not easily discernible, it is best to draw the "stars" on the fabric before beginning embroidery.

Work an 8-pointed star in a counterclockwise motion beginning at 9 o'clock. Bring needle to right side at 9, insert needle at center, bring needle out again between 7 and 8 o'clock and re-enter at center. Continue in this manner until there are 8 points.

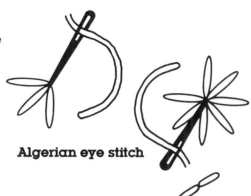

Algerian eye stitch

BACK STITCH

The back stitch is used as the basis for many other stitches and it functions well as an outline stitch.

Bring needle to right side along design line, take a small stitch backward along line, and bring needle to right side again in front of first stitch a stitch length away. Continue along the design line, always finishing stitch by inserting needle at point where last stitch began. On even-weave fabrics, the same number of threads should be covered by each stitch.

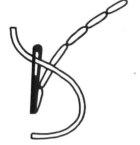

Back stitch

BASTING STITCH

Use the basting stitch for padding scallops or other raised areas. It is worked in the same way as the running stitch, but the stitches alternate long and short.

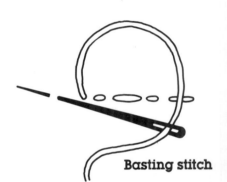

Basting stitch

BLANKET STITCH

The blanket stitch usually is considered a finishing stitch for edges, but it also can be used for outlining when worked small. The blanket stitch has a number of variations, of which the best known is the buttonhole stitch.

Bring needle to right side at A and insert above right at B. Bring needle to right side again at C, with thread under tip of needle, and pull thread through. Continue stitching in this manner, with last point of stitch always acting as first point of next stitch. To finish the blanket stitch, insert needle next to loop (2).

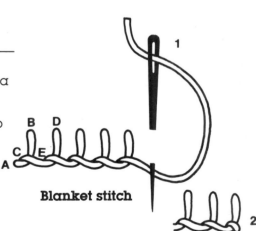

Blanket stitch

BULLION STITCH

The bullion stitch works well for a flower petal or leaf in tiny motifs. It can be used as filling when stitches are worked close together.

Take a back stitch the desired size of the bullion stitch without pulling thread through. Twist the thread around the tip of the needle enough times

to equal the length of the back stitch. Hold the coiled thread down with the left thumb and draw the needle through the coil. Then use the point of the needle to even the coils. Insert needle at point where needle was first inserted for back stitch and pull thread through, leaving coils behind. To make releasing coils easier, use a needle with a small eye.

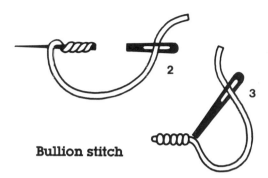

Bullion stitch

BUTTONHOLE STITCH

The buttonhole stitch is blanket stitches worked close together to form a sturdy edge. Like the blanket stitch, it has many variations. It is most frequently used for cutwork embroidery and scalloped edges and, of course, buttonholes.

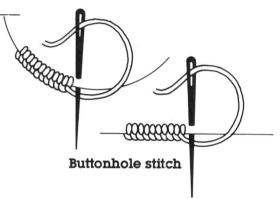

Buttonhole stitch

CHAIN STITCH

The chain stitch is useful both for outlining and for filling.

Draw (or imagine) a line to be covered. Bring thread to right side along line and hold down with left thumb. Insert needle where it last exited and bring point out a short distance away along line, with thread under tip of needle. Continue, always keeping the working thread beneath tip of needle.

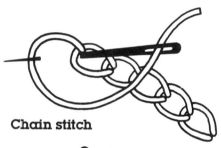

Chain stitch

CHINESE STITCH

Also known as the Pekinese stitch, the Chinese stitch is useful for outlining and for creating decorative borders.

Begin by covering lines to be embroidered with simple back stitch. Exchange needle for a tapestry needle. Lace thread of same or contrasting color through laid stitches, but do not catch fabric in lacing. Laced thread may be pulled tight or left loose (but even), depending upon the look desired.

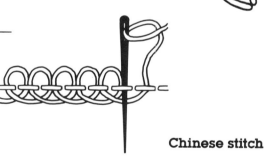

Chinese stitch

FEATHER STITCH

The feather stitch is normally used as a border along edges and hems, and it is also popular for smocking.

To work the feather stitch, it is helpful to mark the center line for easy reference. The stitch is composed of a series of loops alternating from right to left. Bring thread to right side at center (A), insert needle to the right of center (B) and bring needle out below at center (C) with thread under point of needle. Repeat for the left side of the stitch: insert needle to the left of center (D) and bring needle out below center with thread under point of needle. Continue alternating from right to left, and complete the feather stitch by taking a small stitch across last loop.

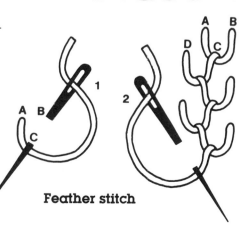

Feather stitch

13

FLY STITCH

The fly stitch is similar to the basic feather stitch. It can be used as a border when worked in a horizontal row, or as a filler when it's scattered.

Bring needle to right side. Hold thread with left thumb and insert needle to the right of the point where thread came out without pulling thread through. Bring needle out below last point of insertion but to center of stitch, and pull thread through with thread under tip of needle. Tack loop in place with tiny stitch.

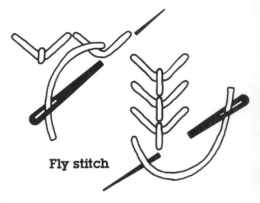

Fly stitch

FRENCH KNOT

Use the French knot to add texture to embroidery. It is a raised stitch which can be used singly for a flower center or an eye, or in a cluster for nubby animal fur. Take care that the embroidery hoop doesn't flatten French knots which have already been worked. Read about embroidery hoops on page 4 for more information.

Bring needle to right side. Hold thread taut with left hand, and wrap thread around point of needle twice. Pull thread tight around needle, and insert needle where it came out, holding thread taut to form a clean knot. You can make larger knots by adding more twists of thread around needle.

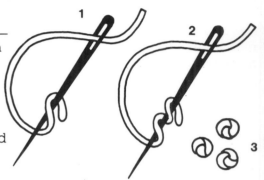

French knot

OVERCASTING STITCH

Overcasting prevents a raw edge from fraying, thus is more often used as a functional sewing stitch than as a decorative embroidery stitch. Since it is mentioned in the directions for several of the projects in this book, we're including the instructions for it here.

Bring needle to right side about 3 or 4 threads from fabric's edge. Wrap thread over edge and bring thread to right side again about 3 or 4 threads away from first stitch and 3 or 4 threads from edge. To prevent curling the fabric, keep spacing and tension even.

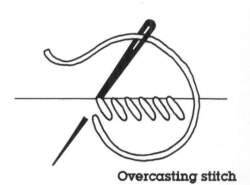

Overcasting stitch

OVERCAST STITCH

See STRAIGHT OVERCAST STITCH.

OUTLINE STITCH

See STEM STITCH.

PEKINESE STITCH

See CHINESE STITCH.

RUNNING STITCH

Among other things, the running stitch is used for quilting. It is an effective embroidery stitch as well.

Bring needle to right side and work from right to left, picking up the same number of threads for each stitch. You can pick up several stitches on the needle before the thread is pulled through if the fabric is not too heavy.

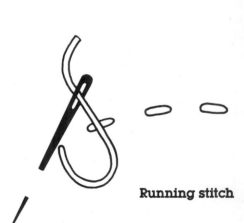

Running stitch

SATIN STITCHES

The satin stitch family includes the most popular stitches for filling solid areas of embroidery. The main objective with a satin stitched design is to work flat, even, smooth stitches which completely cover the fabric underneath. The best results will be obtained when only one or two strands of floss are used.

Basic satin stitch

Begin by bringing needle out at lower side of band to be covered. Insert needle directly above point where needle came out of fabric and pull thread through. Work next stitch beside first, beginning at lower side of design band. An even satin stitch will be achieved by using a stabbing motion with the needle rather than going from one side of the band to the other in a continuous motion. Take care to make a good edge and not to make stitches too long.

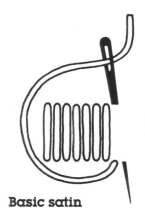

Basic satin

Long and short satin stitch

The name is misleading since, in reality, only the first and last rows of a block of long and short satin stitch are long and short. However, the name is correct in implying that the stitches are taken in varying lengths and/or they have the appearance of being long and short. When worked well, the stitch produces a shaded effect and brings dimension to a design. Before beginning, determine the direction stitches will take within a given shape. On a leaf, for example, the stitches would run diagonally upward from either side of the vein line. The petals of a flower would all radiate separately from the flower's center. The direction of the long and short satin stitch is of prime importance since the flat field it produces will reflect light accordingly.

In the first row, alternate long and short stitches along the perimeter of the area to be filled. In subsequent rows, work long stitches, always piercing the end of the stitch above. Fill in last row with short satin stitches. Take care always to blend stitches well by changing colors with change of row.

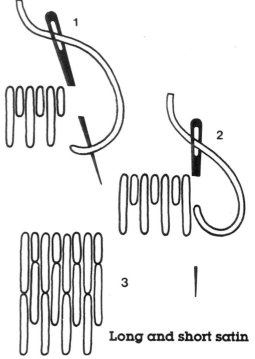

Long and short satin

Slanted satin stitch

This is a good version for working curved bands of embroidery, such as monograms.

First, establish the angle of the slant. It is best to make it ever so slightly diagonal since you will tend to make it flatter and flatter as you progress. Take initial slanted stitch and work outward along band of design. When work to that side is complete, return to point of beginning stitch and work outward from that side. To prevent flattening the angle, take care to insert needle exactly next to preceding stitch at upper edge of band and slightly away from preceding stitch at lower edge of band.

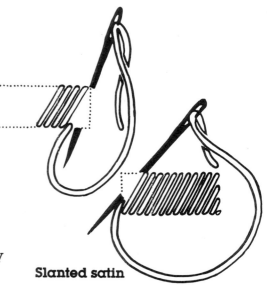

Slanted satin

Padded satin stitch

To add dimension to a design feature, you may want to use padded satin stitch.

To pad, first work outline of design in split or chain stitch. Next, carefully cover design with a horizontal satin stitch, working just to outside edge of padded outline stitching. Then, slowly work satin stitch over design again in any direction other than the horizontal already used.

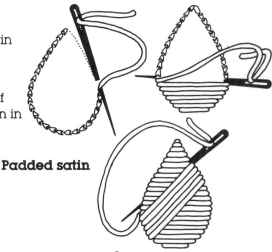

Padded satin

Straight stitch (or Single satin stitch)

Scatter this stitch about for an open filling, or use it to cover straight design lines. It can be worked in any direction and to any length. Take care not to make the stitches too long or to carry the thread too far across the back of the fabric.

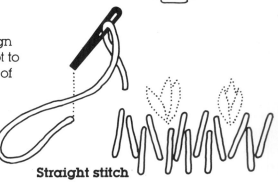

Straight stitch

SEEDING STITCH

This stitch is very simple, yet has many personalities. Scatter it heavily to achieve a shaded effect. Work all stitches in one direction and it produces a uniform filling. Sprinkle it around for a lacy filling. It can be worked singly or in pairs.

To make the seeding stitch, take small straight stitches of equal length.

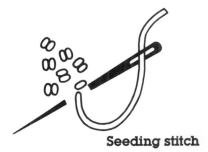

Seeding stitch

SHEAF STITCH

This detached filling stitch earned its title because of its resemblance to a tied bundle of wheat. Sheaves may be scattered, worked in alternating rows, or worked in close horizontal rows.

Work 3 satin stitches close together, bringing needle out at center of third stitch. Then wrap thread around stitch bundles twice (the overcasting stitch) without catching the fabric in the stitches. Bring needle through to the wrong side of fabric under bundle, and continue to next bundle. You can use contrasting thread to "tie" bundles.

Sheaf stitch

SPLIT STITCH

Used either for outlining or filling, it creates a fine flat surface.

Bring needle to right side along design line, insert needle a short distance away and bring needle out again, piercing end of previous stitch. Shorten stitch length slightly on curves to make them smoother.

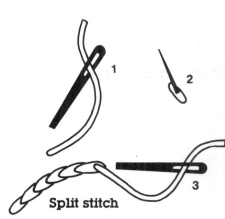

Split stitch

STAR STITCH (or DOUBLE CROSS STITCH)

Scatter it for a filling stitch, or place it in rows to form a decorative border.

Simply put, it is a cross which has been crossed. Bring needle out to right side and take a diagonal stitch. Bring needle out directly below end of stitch and take another diagonal stitch across center of first diagonal. Bring needle out at midpoint of two lower points of star, and cross center. Complete the star by bringing needle out at side midpoint then crossing center. The result should be a star contained in a perfect square.

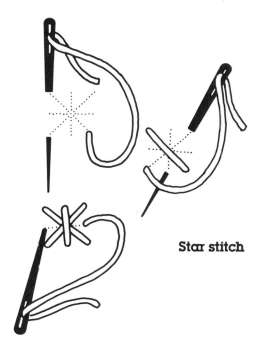

Star stitch

STEM STITCH

Outline with this favorite stitch, or use it to cover lines within a design. It was probably given its name because it was so popular for working stems in floral designs.

Working along a line, bring needle out to right side. Insert needle along line to right, then bring needle back out half a stitch length back. For a wider stitch, angle the needle slightly. Shorten stitches for curves.

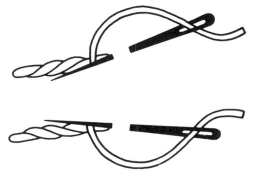

Stem stitch

STRAIGHT STITCH

See SATIN STITCHES.

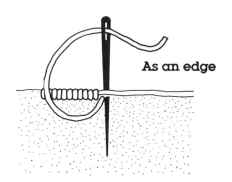

As an edge

STRAIGHT OVERCAST STITCH

A stitch known by many names—overcast, straight overcast, trailing—it is used as a napkin edge finish, and often called by that name, because it makes such a strong and clean edge. It needn't always be worked on an edge, however; it's a good outline stitch as well.

First, lay a well-twisted, round padding thread along edge or design line to be embroidered. Keeping needle in a vertical position, insert needle about 2 threads from edge or design line, exit about 2 threads to other side of design line (and padding thread) if you're not embroidering an edge, and insert the needle next to previous stitch. Continue adding stitches side by side to give a corded effect.

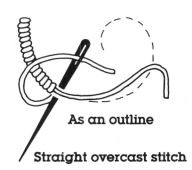

As an outline

Straight overcast stitch

17

WEAVING STITCH

Create a basket-like texture with this stitch.

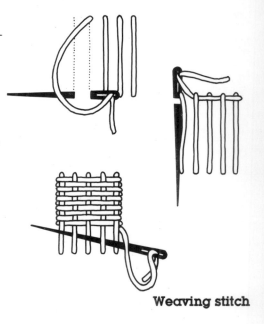

First lay parallel lengthwise threads (straight stitches) longer than ordinary embroidery stitches since they will be anchored later with horizontal stitches. To avoid damaging vertical threads or accidentally piercing fabric, use a tapestry needle to weave in the horizontal threads. Weave in and out of vertical threads, entering and exiting fabric only at ends of rows. Use a contrasting color of thread for weaving if you wish.

Weaving stitch

1 ON THE EDGE

The modest blanket stitch can be very elegant. When worked close together along an edge it becomes the buttonhole stitch. The loop along its edge is resistant to wear, a good quality for a buttonhole to have.

All the beautiful edges on the preceding page use the simple buttonhole stitch to create a never-ending variety of scallops. Scallops are not difficult to embroider, but must be worked with great precision on a tightly woven fabric. And they look best with some basting stitches or a strand of thread underneath to give them a padded appearance.

Have a look at the edges that follow and think of an edge you'd like to decorate—a curtain, the hem of a skirt, a collar, a pillow . . . a buttonhole?

The designs for the scalloped edges on the preceding page are shown full size on the opposite page.

To make a template for scallops, first fold a sheet of paper like a fan into scallop widths, keeping edges perfectly aligned. Decide the depth of the scallop and at that depth draw a line parallel to the edge of the paper. Mark the center of the scallop width, sketch a perfect curve (you can use a compass), and cut through all thicknesses. Open the paper to make a row of perfectly matched scallops. Use that sheet as a pattern for cutting a template of lightweight cardboard (a shoebox works well). Cut design from carton with an X-acto knife. To keep scallops uniform, stop your template at the center or peak of a scallop rather than at the end.

Use a quilting marker or chalk to trace carefully around the template. Plan to end designs at corners, where you will need a special curve to accommodate the junction of the two rows.

To prepare for embroidery, draw the interior line with a second template prepared the same way as the template for the exterior line. Or, pull exterior template in slightly, and trace again.

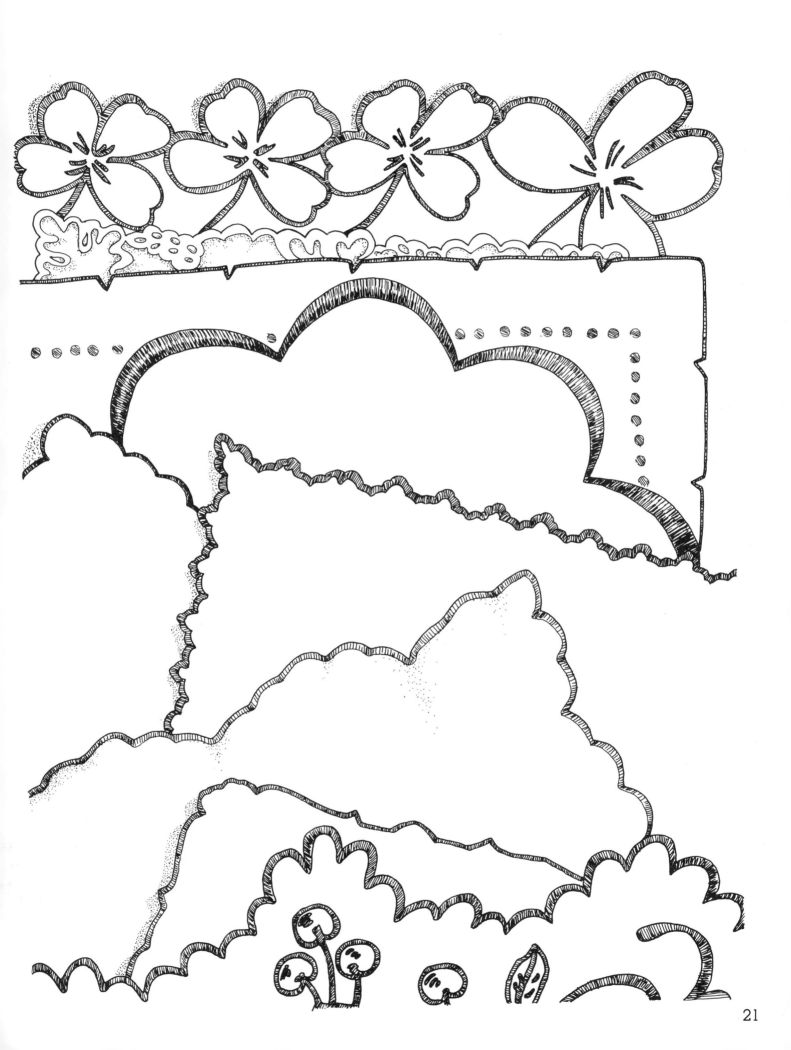

BILLOWY COMFORTER AND PILLOW

An ordinary white pillowcase and sheet become Sunday fare when giant scallops are added to the edges. A European-style pillowcase shows scallops to their best advantage since it opens in the back rather than at the end. But, if you don't have one of those, a standard pillowcase will do just as well.

The comforter case is essentially a big pillowcase made a little larger than the comforter. If the comforter is filled with down, it needs room to expand and fluff up.

When calculating the size of your cases, remember to add a border of equal width to all four sides beyond the actual dimensions needed to cover the pillow or comforter. In addition, allow 2" (5cm) extra fabric, to be trimmed away after embroidery.

After you complete your heirloom, treat it as such. Give it a thorough pressing with a little starch. **Photos: pages 22-23.**

WHAT YOU'LL NEED

White cotton fabric—enough for double the size of the pillowcase and double the size of the comforter cover

DMC Shaded Floss, 2 to 3 skeins of each color: Green 101 and Rose 62

HERE'S HOW:

- **Transfer** design to edges of case;
- **padstitch** (running stitch is fine for padding here) several rows through both layers of fabric, using same color floss that will be used to embroider;

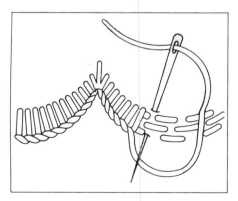

- **use** 1 or 2 strands thread and work blanket stitch along design lines, working from left to right: the thread placed outside the line is held under the thumb of the left

hand; the needle enters at the top and comes out at the bottom of the scallop, passing through the thread to form a loop, the thread is then pulled taut, but not so tight that it gathers the fabric;

- **trim away** fabric from outside edge of scallop with fine pointed scissors after scallop is complete. ■

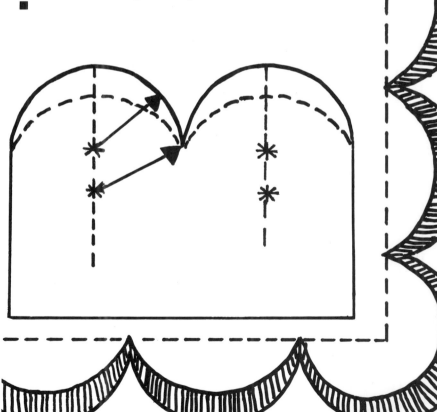

24

ANIMAL HOT PADS

In India, where serving tea is a daily routine, an attractive hot pad is a must for holding the teapot. The rabbit is straight from India; we just added a few companions.

Essentially, these hot pads are made of two identical stuffed animals that have been joined along their spines. They are sewn totally by hand. **Photo: pages 26-27.**

WHAT YOU'LL NEED

6" (15cm) of 36" (90cm) wide cotton per hot pad

DMC Floss, 1 skein of each color: For cat—Black and Red; for rabbit—Blue and Black; for bird—Green, Red, Yellow, and Black; for squirrel—Red, Blue, and Black

HERE'S HOW:

- **Trace** each design and transfer to fabric 4 times, but do not cut out yet;
- **embroider** interior design lines on the 2 outer sides of animal with stem stitch;
- **cut out** designs, adding ½" for seam allowance;
- **stitch** each pair with wrong sides together (1 side of each pair is embroidered and 1 side is plain), turn right side out and join edges with a close blanket stitch along design line, leave about 2" (5cm) open along animal's back for stuffing;
- **stuff** animal well;
- **trim away** edge of fabric close to blanket stitch and close the opening with blanket stitch;
- **join** the pair of stuffed animals with a slip stitch, beginning at the beak or nose, and continuing along the back and down to the tail. Use same color thread as that used for the blanket stitch. ■

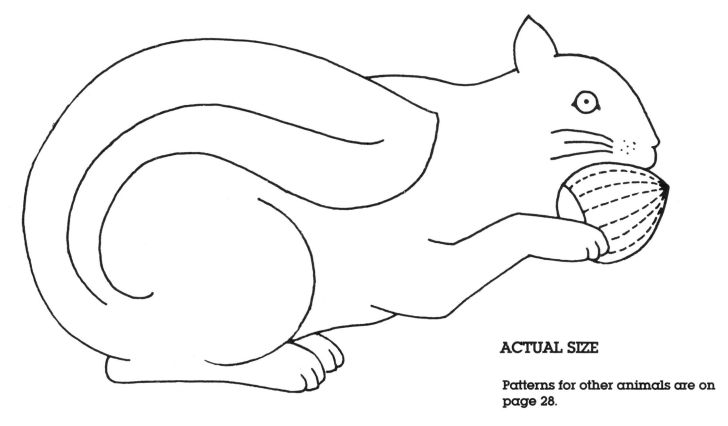

ACTUAL SIZE

Patterns for other animals are on page 28.

ANIMAL HOT PADS, continued from page 25.

ACTUAL SIZE

ALL IN THE BUTTONHOLES

Your favorite vest may be in great shape, except for its buttonholes. Don't despair, give it a new life by replacing the buttons and reworking the buttonholes all in different colors of floss, using—what else?—the buttonhole stitch!

Making a beautiful buttonhole is less mystifying than it appears. The five steps shown here tell you how to make a perfect buttonhole every time. And a machine-made buttonhole can't hold a candle to a carefully stitched handmade buttonhole.

Our buttonhole stitch is worked over an existing buttonhole, thus it must be larger than normal. To rework a buttonhole, start with step 4 of the directions. We added a contrasting sheaf stitch at each end. **Photos: page 30.**

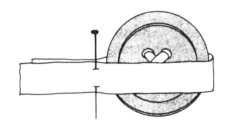

1 Determine the size of the buttonhole by measuring the button, then add ⅛" (3mm) for flat buttons and ¼" (6mm) for thick buttons.

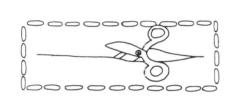

2 Make a running stitch to indicate the finished size of the buttonhole. Clip it open with fine pointed scissors.

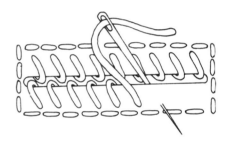

3 Overcast the raw edges to prevent raveling.

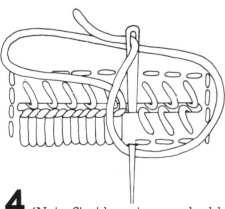

4 (Note: Start here to rework old buttonholes.) **Work** the buttonhole stitch, covering the running stitch. You can start from either direction.

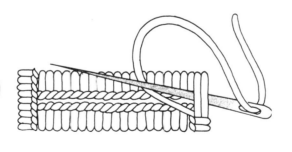

5 Secure the ends by squaring off with more buttonhole stitches.

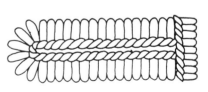

Or, **fan out** the stitches on the end under the most stress.

2 LIVELY BED LINENS

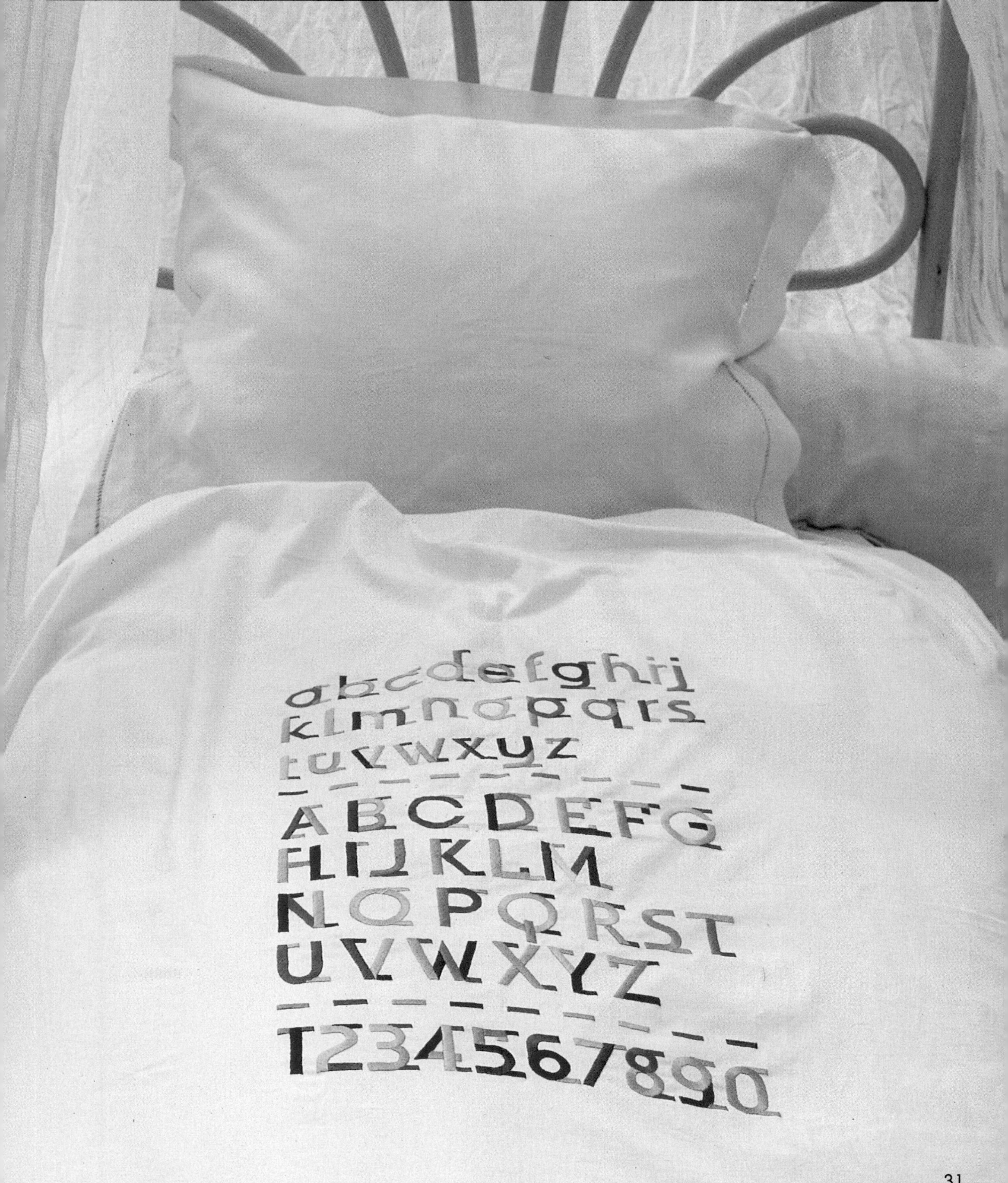

2 LIVELY BED LINENS

A wide field of plain cotton is an embroiderer's dream. Bed linens have intrigued thread artists for centuries with their wide-open spaces so conveniently displayed.

Try your hand at creating a personalized set of sheets and pillowcases. You can decorate purchased linens or buy cotton sheeting from a fabric store. In this chapter, there's something special for the man of the house, for baby, and for anyone else who'd appreciate a set of custom sheets. But don't stop here—many other designs in this book would make attractive decorations for bed linens.

When you transfer the designs, consider placing them fairly deep on the top of the sheet. Then, when the covers are turned back, the embroidery will stand out beautifully!

FOR WOMEN OF LETTERS

You don't have to be Emily Bronte or Gail Godwin to be a woman of letters. Replace the pen with a needle, and write in thread. The alphabet shown here is very modern, and sewn in dynamic colors. There's a secret behind the beautiful, even stitching: it's satin stitch worked on the diagonal! Note the illustration here. Since most letters are curved, working on the diagonal will make your work faster and more uniform. **Photo: page 31.**

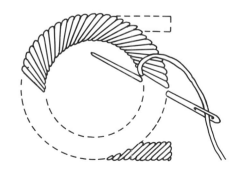

The photograph of the alphabet on the following pages provides a full-size illustration of each letter as well as a good look at the stitching technique and coloring. Use no more than two strands of floss, and choose fabric that deserves such effort.

If you would like to embroider the letters in a smaller size, as the photograph below illustrates, take advantage of the services a copy shop can provide. A printed page can usually be reproduced at a smaller size for only pennies. To embroider smaller letters, use stem stitch and a single strand of floss. You don't have to use all twenty-six letters, of course. Just a few initials on a pocket can make a tremendous difference in the look of a dress or shirt. To monogram a pocket which has already been sewn to a garment, take the pocket off the garment, back it with a lightweight fabric large enough to fit your embroidery hoop, and embroider. Then trim away excess backing fabric and remount the pocket as if it had always been monogrammed.

Grade-schoolers delight in reciting the alphabet. Why not place the letters right around the hem of a six-year-old's dress?

a b c d e f g h i j

k l m n o p q r s

t u v w x y z

A B C D E F G

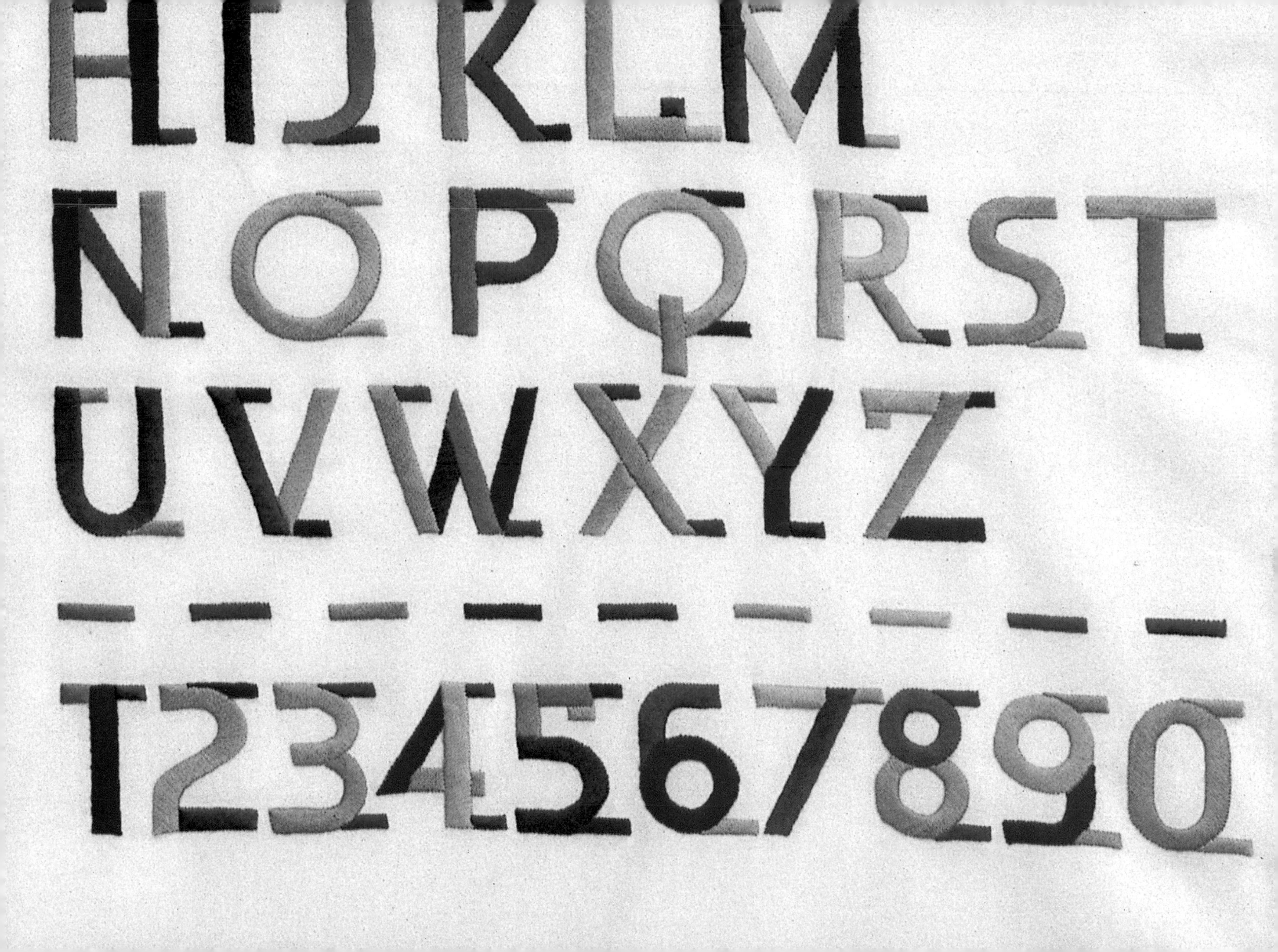

HIJKLM
NOPQRST
UVWXYZ
- - - - -
1234567890

TALENTED TEDDY ALPHABET

This talented boy and teddy bear have managed to form all twenty-six letters of the alphabet! You can use this alphabet to monogram pajamas or robes, or you can have it enlarged so the letters will fit quilt blocks. If you use the alphabet at the size shown here or in a smaller size, it might be best to work the boy's pajamas in a solid color, or simply to outline them, rather than to make them striped.

FOR DREAMERS

Many people find their best ideas come to them as they sleep. For many, that's the only time the mind is allowed to wander at random. There are those who believe the brain can absorb recorded sounds during sleep. Then perhaps it's also true that the bed linens which swaddle you can affect your dreams. Even if they don't, isn't there a unique satisfaction in ending each day surrounded by your own beautiful handiwork?

The bouquets shown here on a white cotton sheet and pillowcase are embroidered in long and short satin stitch. All motifs are the same in design and coloration. If you prefer more variety, you can change or alternate the colors of each bouquet. **Photo: page 38.**

WHAT YOU'LL NEED

Coats and Clark Floss, 1 skein of each color:
Greens—240 (a), 208 (b), 261 (c); Yellows—292 (d), 293 (e), 300 (f), 301 (g), 311 (h); Beiges—885 (i), 386 (j); Pinks—06 (k), 08 (l), 01 (m), 024 (n), 036 (o), 337 (p), 1201 (q); Reds—028 (r), 033 (s).

HERE'S HOW:

- **Transfer** motif (shown full size here) to pillowcases and sheets;
- **place** fabric in hoop and embroider with 3 strands floss, using basic and long and short satin stitches following lines within petals to indicate color changes. ∎

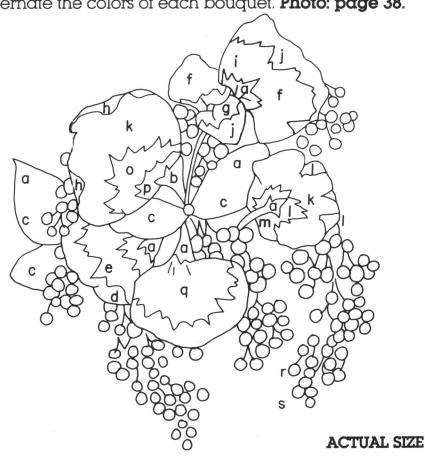

ACTUAL SIZE

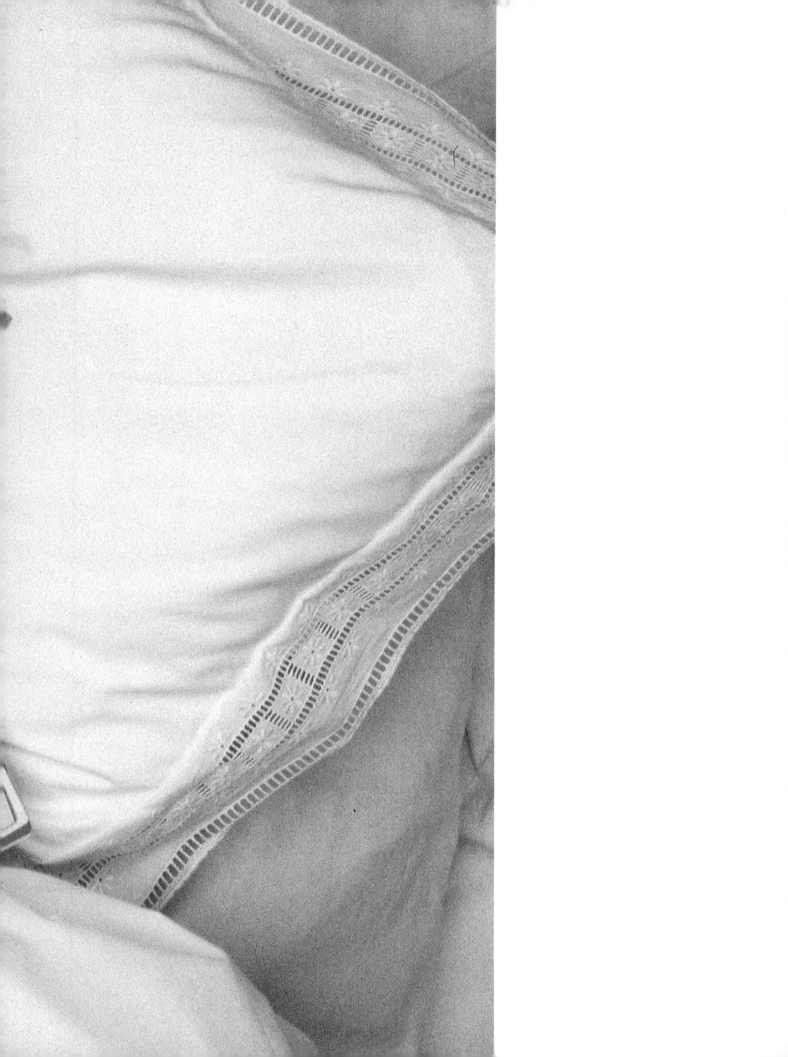

PILLOWS FOR A DAY BED

When sheer laziness puts you on your back, you'll doze more peacefully on these relaxing sketches by David Hockney. Any simple line drawing is appropriate for embroidering, and naturally, you may have your own favorite artist—even comic strips offer endless possibilities. The four David Hockney sketches are all here to be transferred and quickly embroidered with your favorite outline stitch. You may choose from stem, backstitch, chain, or split stitch. **Photo: pages 42-43.**

Enlarge these sketches to fit your pillows.

PILLOWS FOR A DAY BED,
continued from page 41

Enlarge these sketches to fit your pillows.

A DUCKY QUILT

If your best friend has just had a baby and you have no time for a demanding project right now, this colorful crib set may solve your problem. It's embroidered with four strands of crochet cotton in giant running stitches.

The whole project is quick! The designs are embroidered on a bleached muslin rectangle first, then stripes of bias tape are added, and finally the quilt is sewn together like a pillow. Top, backing, and batting are sewn with right sides together, turned, and slipstitched closed. Easy quilting outlines the animal characters to make the designs pop out.

What are you waiting for? Get the gift wrap ready! **Photo: page 46.**

WHAT YOU'LL NEED

For the Quilt

(Finished quilt measures 38" x 48" or 96cm x 122cm)

3 yds (3m) 45" (115cm) wide bleached cotton muslin

Crib-size quilt batting

Single fold bias tape: 1 pkg each pink and orange, 2 pkgs each lime, turquoise, and lavender

For the Pillow

(Finished pillow is 7½" x 10" or 19cm x 25½cm)

½ yd bleached cotton muslin

Fiberfill for pillow stuffing

Single fold bias tape: 1 pkg any color indicated above for the quilt

For Embroidery

DMC Floss: 1 skein Black

1 ball each of Crochet Cotton (Art. #42) by Belding Lily: Pink 43, Light Blue 26, Emerald Green 62, Glo-Tone (Lime Green) 55, Yellow 10, Radiant Blue (Turquoise) 170, Dark Orange 21, Red 95

Washable quilting marker

Darning needle #1

Felt-tip pen

HERE'S HOW:

- **Trace** embroidery motifs (on page 133) onto tissue paper and go over design with felt-tip pen on both sides of paper;

- **place** motif under muslin and trace in position shown on quilt diagram—to reverse designs, simply flip paper and trace;

- **work** designs in running stitch using 4 strands of crochet cotton—thread 2 strands through the needle and knot the end to make 4 strands—making stitches on right side of fabric longer than on wrong side;

- **use** 2 strands of crochet cotton and satin stitch for solid areas such as beaks, feet, glowworm stripes, and butterfly dots;

- **work** the duck's back foot in stem stitch;

- **work** eyes in French knots with black floss;

- **make** designs on pillow stand out: place batting between embroidered fabric and an extra piece of fabric, quilt around design, and complete pillow as usual. ■

QUILT DIAGRAM

R = RED   T = RADIANT BLUE
P = PINK   G = EMERALD GREEN
Y = YELLOW   L = GLO-TONE (LIME)
B = LIGHT BLUE O = DARK ORANGE

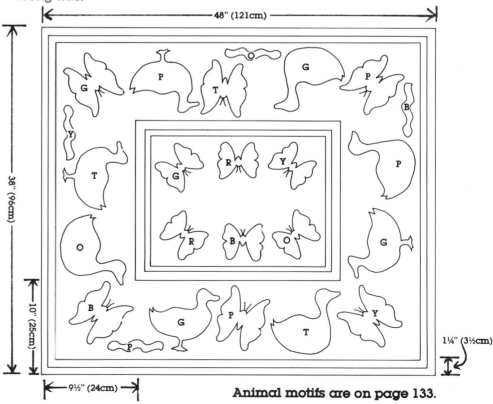

48" (121cm)

38" (96cm)

10" (25cm)

9½" (24cm)

1¼" (3½cm)

Animal motifs are on page 133.

3 UNUSUAL BEGINNINGS

Who says embroidery designs must come from embroidery design books and be worked in embroidery floss? Nobody! But many people believe it just the same.

Have you ever considered embroidering on a basket? Or on the seat of an oak splint chair? A window screen? These surfaces are all woven, and all could be embroidered. With the right thread (you probably wouldn't want to use six-stranded floss) the results can be sensational!

This chapter challenges you to put embroidery in unusual places and to work with uncommon materials. Many of the projects may surprise you. Ever thought of embroidering on a shoe?

THE COVER

Our cover photo illustrates a completely unregulated style of embroidery which is also an edging. It was an ordinary box of children's crayons that inspired the revival of this old blouse.

Here is a project dedicated especially to all you doodlers, only this doodle shouldn't be thrown away when it's finished!

It's easy! Use Brilliant Embroidery and Cutwork Thread in soft and shaded colors. Work the straight stitch along the edge of a collar (or any edge you like) in varying depths, and change colors each time your needle runs out of thread. The stars that fall from the collar are worked in the same colors in Algerian eye stitch. **Photo: page 47.**

BADGES

The mother and son on page 51 are attentive, cautious, quiet, patient and they are lovers of nature. For that reason they enjoy adorning their clothes with badges to share their appreciation of nature with others. Their embroidered bird designs come from their own meticulous sketches, but if you're not a patient artist, you can cheat a little. Pick up a bird book from your local library—one with colored pictures, of course—and transfer your favorite feathered friend to a piece of white felt. If the size is smaller than you would like, enlarge the picture at a copy shop. Here are some terrific animal designs—any one of them would look great embroidered on a cap or coat sleeve.

Your own badge doesn't have to be an animal, and it doesn't have to be embroidered first on felt. Embroider something about yourself—there's something special in all of us. **Photo: pages 50-51.**

BADGES, continued from page 49

MALLARD DUCK

WHAT YOU'LL NEED _____

Circle of white felt (2mm/15 oz.
weight; 12" (30cm) in diameter)
Note: Silk thread looks best.

DMC Floss—a skein per color
unless otherwise noted:
Beige 644, 613, 437; Tan 436;
Gray 415; Green 472, 988, 319;
Yellow 725; Rust 301; Blue 996,
806; Pale Rose 948; Orange 900;
Black; White; and 2 skeins Dull
Green 936.

HERE'S HOW:

- **If you** are using a hoop, cut out 12" (30cm) circle after embroidery is complete;

- **transfer** duck design to felt;

- **embroider** duck in parts (wings, body, head, beak, tail) in satin stitch using photo as color guide;

- **work** outline stitch along lines using photo as color guide;

- **turn** under ⅜" (1cm) along edge of circle and baste;

- **embroider** a ⅜" (1cm) wide band along edge in straight stitch;

- **applique** felt to clothing or frame it for a wall piece. ■

52

FRESH AND FRUITY CUSHIONS

They're fresh because they're made of grass cloth—like beach mats are made of. Many upholstery supply stores carry it. And they're fruity because they're decorated with plums, pineapples, and grapes. The embroidery "thread" is dyed raffia, the fiber of the raffia palm tree normally used to make baskets.

To dye raffia, just use common household dyes, divide the raffia into small bundles, and dip them in the hot mixture for a matter of two to three minutes. Voila! Beautifully shaded skeins—raffia will not accept dye uniformly! Lucky for you, for with no effort on your part, the shaded raffia creates hollows and bumps that make the fruit look real enough to eat. Some words of caution: work with the raffia while it is still slightly damp and keep it out of sunlight so it will retain the rich colors. **Photo: next page.** (Remaining instructions are on pages 56-57.)

PLUMS

STITCHES: LONG AND SHORT SATIN FOR FRUIT, STRAIGHT FOR LEAVES, AND STEM FOR OUTLINES.

□ = 2"/5cm

FRESH AND FRUITY CUSHIONS, continued from page 53

WHAT YOU'LL NEED

A rectangle of grass cloth for each cushion 23½" (60cm) x 47" (120cm)

A 21" (54cm) pillow form for each cushion

Raffia, 1 6-oz. package for each cushion

Household dyes: dull gold (for plum), golden yellow (for pineapple), deep purple, light purple, and violet (for grapes), and green for all leaves

A blunt-tipped needle with large eye (tapestry needle)

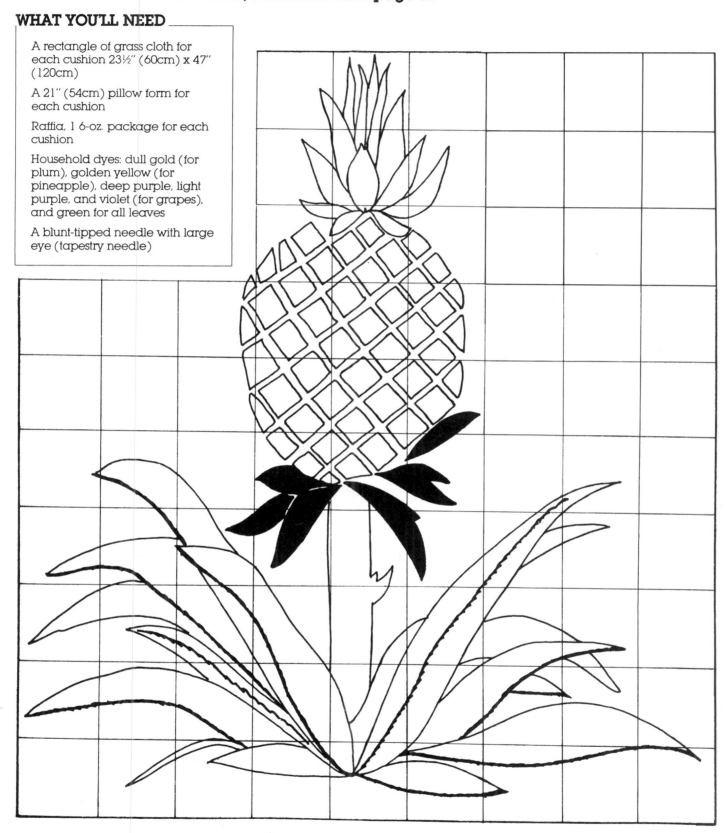

PINEAPPLE

STITCHES: BASIC SATIN FOR FRUIT, STRAIGHT UNDERLINED BY STEM FOR LEAVES, AND STEM FOR OUTLINES.

□ = 2"/5cm

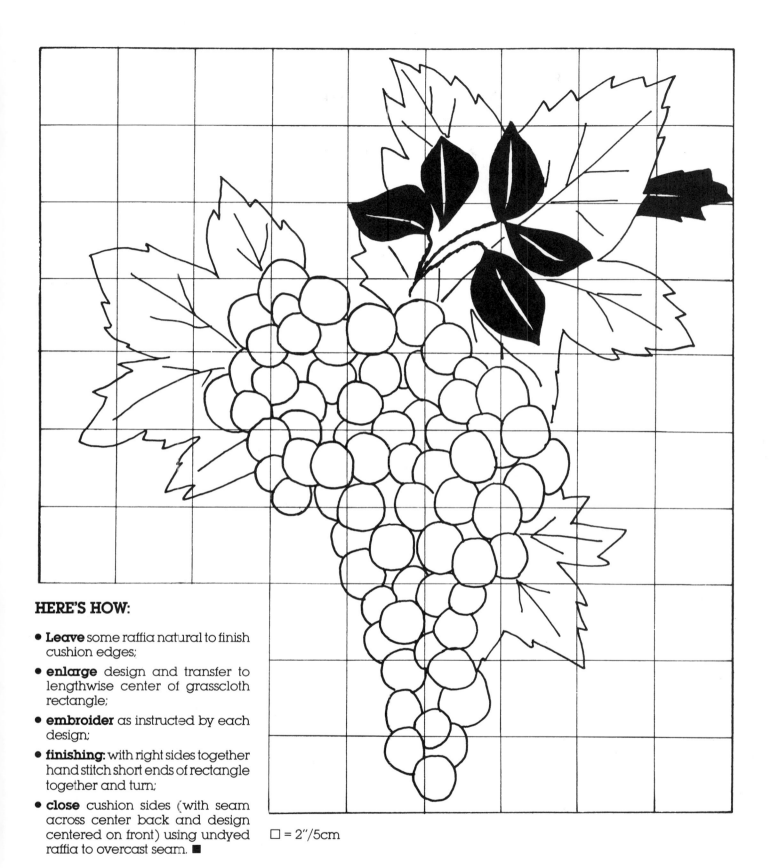

HERE'S HOW:

- **Leave** some raffia natural to finish cushion edges;

- **enlarge** design and transfer to lengthwise center of grasscloth rectangle;

- **embroider** as instructed by each design;

- **finishing:** with right sides together hand stitch short ends of rectangle together and turn;

- **close** cushion sides (with seam across center back and design centered on front) using undyed raffia to overcast seam. ■

☐ = 2"/5cm

GRAPES

STITCHES: STRAIGHT FOR FRUIT, STEM FOR VEINS AND OUTLINES OF LARGE LEAVES, AND STRAIGHT OUTLINED BY STEM FOR SMALL LEAVES.

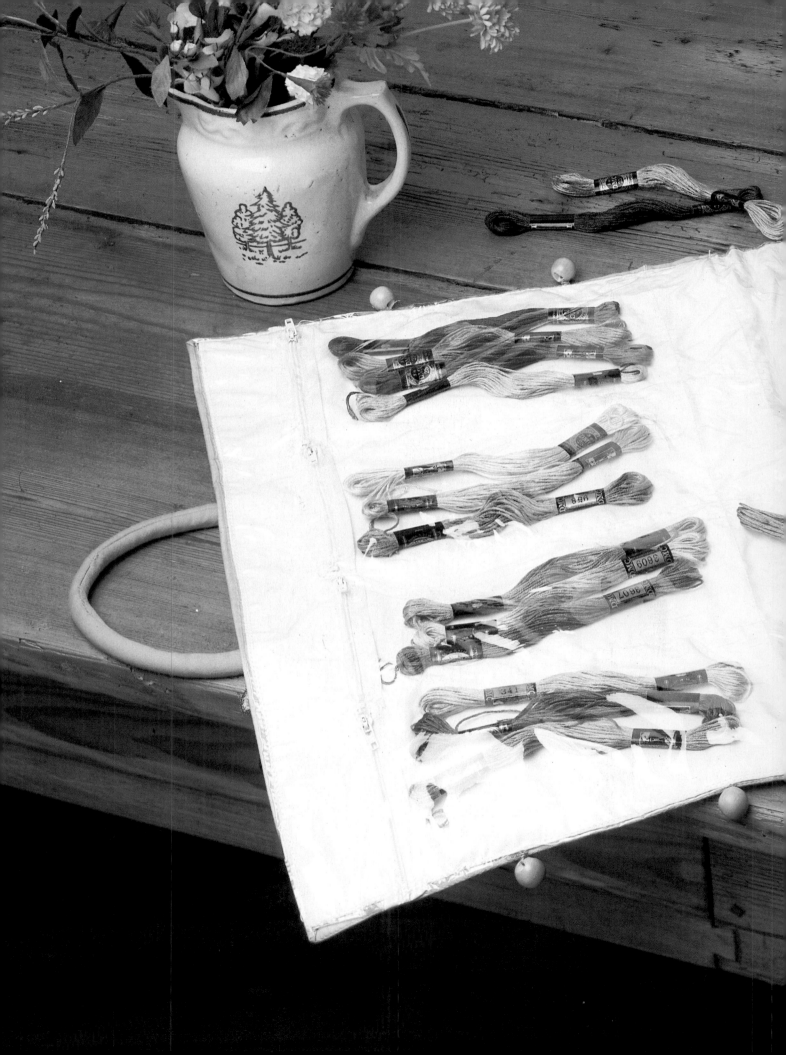

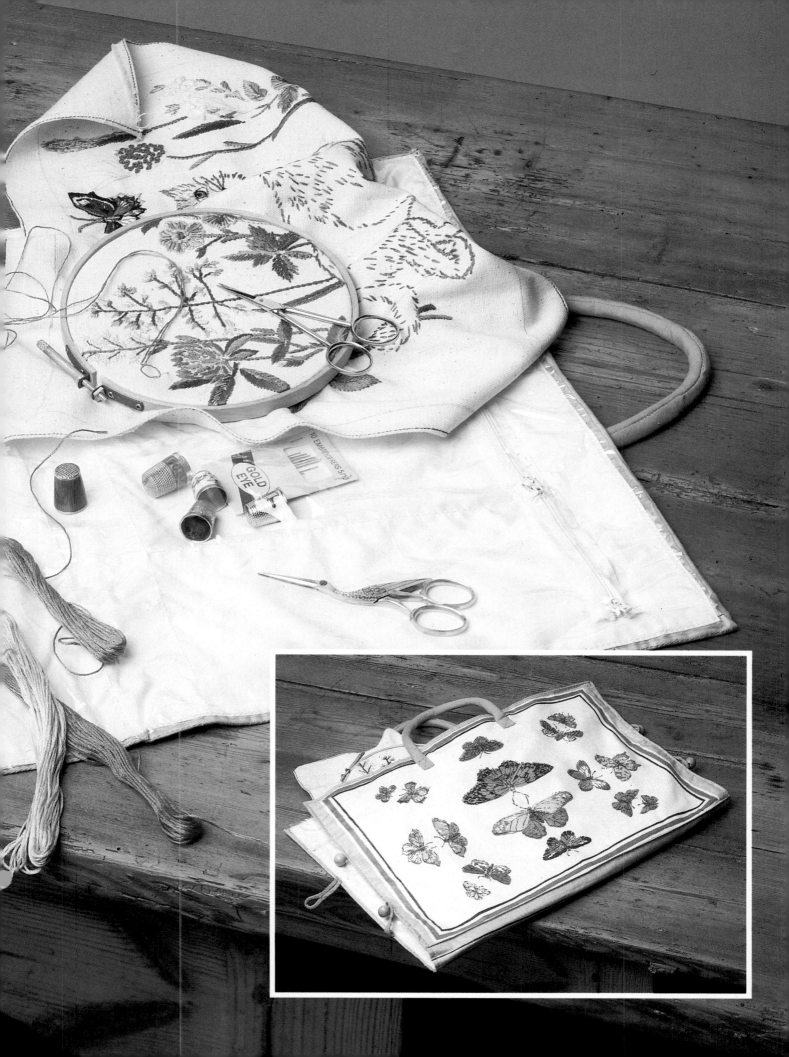

A CASE FOR EMBROIDERY

Tired of fumbling around in a bottomless bag to find your embroidery supplies? Try this compact embroiderer's valise with eight see-through pockets. It's a great way to organize your materials and those luscious skeins so they're visible. Your current embroidery project will be neatly packed up and ready to go with you at a moment's notice. **Photo: pages 58-59.**

WHAT YOU'LL NEED

½ yd (½m) of each of following materials:
cotton for cover
cotton for lining
clear plastic

1 pkg ¾" (2cm) hem facing

Eight 7" zippers

4 ball buttons

¾ yd (70cm) cording

HERE'S HOW:

- **Cut** all three materials into rectangles 17½" x 25" (45cm x 64cm);
- **press under** ½" (1cm) along edges of cover rectangle and ¾" (2cm) along edges of lining rectangle;

- **assemble** zipper lengths: cut zippers to 4" (10cm) lengths, slipstitch ends closed, and stitch bottom of one zipper to top of another in two bands of four;
- **position** zipper bands under plastic as shown in diagram and stitch along zipper tape;
- **slice** plastic open along zipper teeth and trim away excess plastic from around zipper;
- **position** plastic over lining and stitch along stitching lines indicated in diagram to form pockets;
- **fold under** edges of plastic to inside of pressed lining and topstitch around edges;

- **make** 4 buttonhole loops from hem facing and stitch ends to wrong side of lining, positioning as shown on diagram;
- **cover** two 12" (30cm) lengths of cording with hem facing leaving 1" (2.5cm) at each end free of cording;
- **stitch** the corded handles to right side of cover, positioning as shown on diagram;
- **topstitch** plastic and lining to cover with wrong sides together and handles toward cover;
- **attach** buttons as shown in diagram. ∎

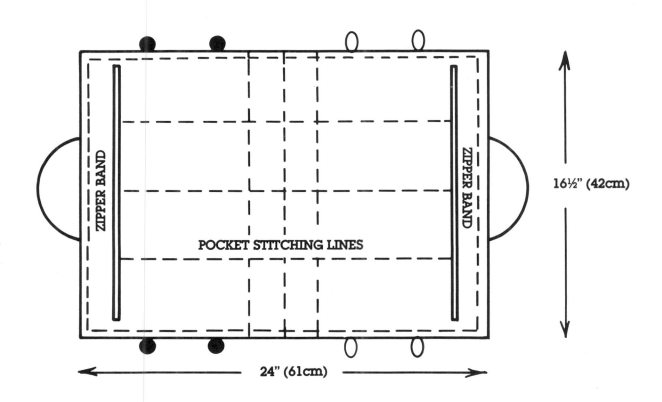

POCKET STITCHING LINES

ZIPPER BAND

ZIPPER BAND

16½" (42cm)

24" (61cm)

EMBROIDERED WINDOWS

The embroidery is the same, the needle is the same, the thread is the same, but metal canvas? Why not? And why not on a window where it's readily seen? Put an end to drab or ugly views.

If you don't want to put screen over glass, how about a cheerful decoration on the screen door to welcome visitors? You have a choice of the four designs here, or you can use other designs shown throughout the book. Since the screen creates a grid, any gridded design would be easy to transfer. You might even consider cross-stitch and/or different colors. **Photo: pages 62-63.**

WHAT YOU'LL NEED

Fine mesh screen

DMC floss — Ecru

Optional: double-faced tape for attaching screen to window

HERE'S HOW:

- **Measure** window, add ½" (1cm) on all sides of measurement, and cut screen to that size with wire cutters;
- **transfer** design to screen center with felt-tip pen;
- **embroider** motif and border in satin stitch;
- **tape or tack** screen to window. ■

□ = 6 strands of wire

THE BORDER

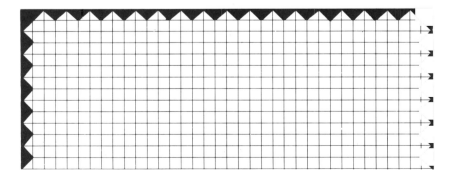

□ = 6 strands of wire

FANCY FEET

Embroidery today is filled with humor. You never know quite where to expect it. On the next page we find a gentle crab clinging to the side of a canvas boot and a friendly starfish sunning on a pair of espadrilles. Neither is very difficult to re-create. **Photo: next page.**

THE STARFISH

WHAT YOU'LL NEED

Pearl Cotton, 1 skein of each color:
Gray-Blue, Ecru, Rose, Sandy Yellow, and Sea Green

HERE'S HOW:

- **Work** shaded sections in straight stitch;
- **work** unshaded sections in French knot or seed stitch using photo as color key.

THE CRAB

WHAT YOU'LL NEED

DMC Floss, 1 skein of each color: Brown, Salmon, Rose, Ecru, Gray, and 3 shades Blue-Green

HERE'S HOW:

- **Work** entire crab in simple straight stitch using 3 strands thread; brown eyes, salmon pinchers, rose legs, and a body in a blend of 6 colors: ecru, rose, gray, and all 3 shades of blue-green. ■

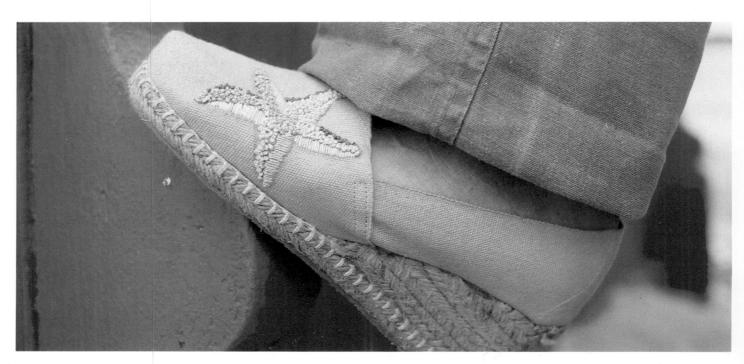

4   FOR THE KIDS

Do you still have a quilt or pillow a doting grandmother made especially for you when you were a child? Such gifts are always cherished. This chapter is dedicated to little ones who make us want to make things for them. There are ideas on the following pages to suit every personality, from the prima donna to the house sheriff. Children will surely appreciate what you embroider for them but will really become your fans if you teach them to embroider for themselves!

CHERRIES ON OVERALLS

Your thoughtful attention will always be rewarded when it's directed toward children, especially when the child is included in the creative process.

Here, two children are wearing some of their most comfortable everyday clothes. The clothes may get dirty, but the bright red cherries hand-stitched onto the bibs will keep shining. Before you start a project for a child, allow him to help choose the design. Then, let him watch and "help" as you embroider. You may start a fan club.

To embroider on purchased overalls, you might have to rip out some seams to make the work area accessible. The pocket on the little girl's jumper, shown here, was unstitched across the pocket top and resewn after embroidering. **Photo: preceding page.**

FOR COLLAR

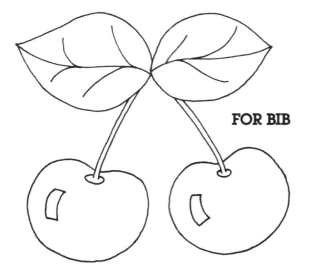

FOR BIB

WHAT YOU'LL NEED

DMC Floss, 1 skein of each color: White, Red (2 shades), and Green

HERE'S HOW:

Fill in with basic satin stitch and work vein lines of leaves with stem or chain stitch. ■

ACTUAL SIZE

BACK-TO-SCHOOL SMOCKS

Summer's over, school buses are everywhere, there are no baseball games in the street anymore, the kids have gone back to school. Some are happy to be back, others watch the clock until the school bell rings to go home.

Why not make going back to school a special event this year with an apron or smock designed specifically for the occasion? You can't dress up little boys for very long, so take advantage of the opportunity while they're still in kindergarten.

Remember how appealing the blackboard looked when you were in primary school? For the most part, it was the teacher's domain. Give children their own blackboards—on their clothes, anyway—made of black hem facing. The chalk tray is tan bias tape and the baseboard is light blue bias tape. The big pieces of furniture, the desk and the plant pot, are appliqued.

They're all there: the teacher, the math student, the quiet little girls, the whisperer, and even the rowdy little boy who got caught. It's the classroom story recounted in satin stitches and bias tape.

If you want a change from satin stitches, try actually braiding the little girls' hair. **Photos: pages 70-71 and 74-75.**

MERIT STAR

WHAT YOU'LL NEED

DMC Floss, 1 skein of each color: Silver, Red, Deep Blue, Gray-Blue

HERE'S HOW:

Work entire design in satin stitch: star and pin in silver, ribbon in red, and center of star in blues. ■

MERIT STAR EMBROIDERY DESIGN

CORAL SHIRT

WHAT YOU'LL NEED

DMC Floss, 1 skein of each color: White, Black, Blue 597, Gray 318, Pink 945, Yellow 782

Bias tape: ⅝ yd (50cm) each gray and brown

6" (15cm) x 4" (10cm) piece of black cotton cut from colorfast bias.

HERE'S HOW:

- **Applique** strip of gray bias tape where you would like young student's feet to be;
- **use** design to position blackboard bias and chalk tray bias, applique them in place;
- **embroider** design in basic satin stitch using photo and your imagination as color keys. ■

EMBROIDERY DESIGN FOR CORAL SHIRT

BACK TO SCHOOL SMOCKS, continued from page 69

BACK TO SCHOOL SMOCKS, continued from page 69

GRAY DRESS

WHAT YOU'LL NEED

DMC Floss, 1 skein of each color: Greens 986, 988, 122, 989, 992, 991, 503; Blues 930, 939, 518, 792, 597, 800, 519, 826, 926; Earth tones 729, 420, 918, 841, 938, 780, 433, 632; Grays 317, 318, 3022; Reds 3685, 326; Yellows 676, 726; Pinks 316, 945; White; Black

Bias tape: 40″ (1m) 1″ wide gray-blue, 1⅝ yds (1.5m) ½″ wide light brown

2″ wide (5cm) colorfast black bias hem facing: 1⅛ yds (1m).

HERE'S HOW:

- **Place and applique** gray-blue bias tape just above dress hemline;

- **place and applique** black band 2⅜″ (6cm) above gray-blue bias tape;

- **applique** brown bias tape (chalk tray) to lower edge of black band;

- **use** photo and actual designs as guides to place desk, trash basket, and flower pot and topstitch or applique them in place (You may want to use brown felt for these furnishings.);

- **use** chalkboard and baseboard as reference points to place designs, work them in satin stitch. ■

EMBROIDERY DESIGN FOR GRAY DRESS

APPLIQUE

72

A_B_C_D_

BLUE PINAFORE

WHAT YOU'LL NEED

DMC Floss, 1 skein of each color: White, Black, Gray 318, Pink 945, Yellow 676, Brown 632, Blue 826

Bias tape: 8" (20cm) pale blue (1" wide), 6" (15cm) brown (½" wide)

6" (15cm) x 4" (10cm) piece of black cotton cut from colorfast bias.

HERE'S HOW:

See "HERE'S HOW" for CORAL SHIRT. ■

EMBROIDERY DESIGN FOR BLUE PINAFORE

ALL DESIGNS ARE ACTUAL SIZE

73

TEACH YOUR CHILD TO EMBROIDER

Young children are generally fascinated with almost anything that adults like to do. Both girls and boys enjoy sewing. When you teach a young child to embroider, remember that his motor skills are not so well-developed as yours, and he will need encouragement.

Go step by step, and start with basics. First, show your young student how to thread a needle with a short length of yarn. Have him use fairly thick yarn, a large needle, and a loosely woven fabric such as burlap. Teach the simplest stitch of all, the running stitch. It's practical and pretty.

Show the child how to make a line of stitches by drawing a line on the fabric for him to follow. After he has learned to stitch in a variety of stitch lengths, draw dots one-quarter inch apart on the fabric, and show him how to follow the dots to make stitches of equal length. Of course, with all that newly acquired skill, the child will want to try a real project. How about a burlap placemat worked in running stitch? You can help by drawing the design on the burlap. After outer border is stitched, pull away loose threads to form a fringe. Your young friend can make one for each member of the family!

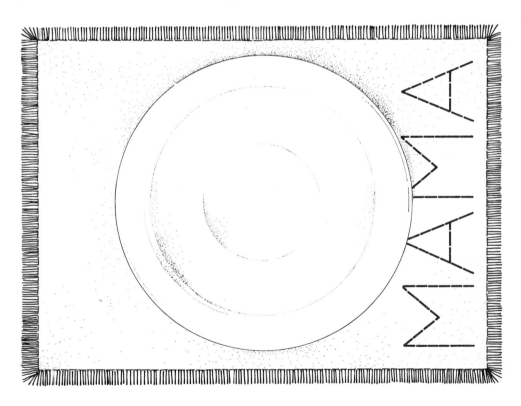

The blanket stitch is a little more difficult than the running stitch. For practice, draw dots about one-quarter inch apart along the edge of a piece of scrap. Demonstrate the stitch, using the dots as reference points for going in and out of the fabric.

Try this mask to let the child practice working blanket stitch. Make the pattern by folding a piece of paper in half and centering the foldline between the child's eyes. Draw outer and inner cutting lines, and trim the pattern accordingly. Allow the child to pin the pattern onto two layers of felt and cut out his mask. Tack the mask pieces together at center, and demonstrate the blanket stitch worked along the edge. When the mask is finished, tack elastic to each side.

A word of advice: let your children choose their own colors. With their uninhibited color sense, they may teach you something!

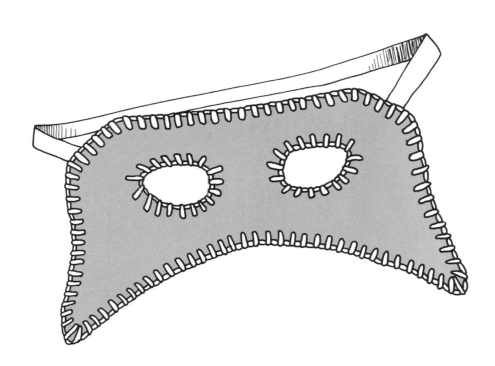

STORYBOOK EMBROIDERY

The well-behaved little girl on the following page is wearing an illustration by Benjamin Rabier from an old children's reader. So often, old illustrations were more graphic than their modern counterparts, making them perfect subjects for embroidery. As for colors, this illustration works up beautifully with just a single color.

Try transferring an illustration from one of your child's favorite stories onto a yoke or a pocket. The work will go quickly in chain or stem stitch. Or, why not embroider the entire story onto a patchwork quilt? **Photo: next page.**

5 JUST FOR FUN

Sheer whimsy. You wouldn't spend hours
embroidering a T-shirt for any other reason!
Embroidery doesn't always have to be serious.

Consider embroidery that tricks the eye.
Whimsical embroidery might easily become
your favorite kind!

TIES THAT TEASE

Create the illusion of a tie, with its knot slipped down so as to not confine the
neck, or a bow tie, amply polka-dotted, thoughtfully stitched in shades of blue and
red. The illusion's success lies in the detail of the design and its careful placement all the
way around the neck. The French call it "trompe l'oeil," tricking the eye. A simple white
T-shirt, a waiter's white jacket, or a pair of overalls are all perfect settings for a little
adornment which can change the whole look of a garment. You might consider a
camera hung from the neck, or a necklace appearing from underneath the collar of a
man's shirt, or a dollar bill slipping out of a jeans pocket.

Our shirts are embroidered in satin stitches outlined by chain stitch. The shading effect is
achieved through using color "families." In the bow tie, for example, three slightly
different shades of blue are used. The shading that results gives the impression of a silky
fabric catching and reflecting the light. **Photo: preceding page.**

HERE'S HOW:

(Note: use 3 strands thread)

- **Enlarge and transfer** design to
  T-shirt (use your imagination for
  back neck);
- **outline** design in chain stitch using
  photo as color key;
- **embroider** dots in basic satin stitch
  using reds and rose threads;
- **outline** dots in chain stitch;
- **fill in** remainder of bow tie (alternating the varying shades of blue)
  using long and short satin stitch;
- **stitch** "pleat" lines with chain stitch
  in royal blue.

WHAT YOU'LL NEED

White cotton T-shirt (pre-shrunk)

DMC Floss, a skein of each color:
Bright Red 817, Orange Red 351,
Peachy Rose 353, Sky Blue 800,
Medium Blue 809, Royal Blue
797

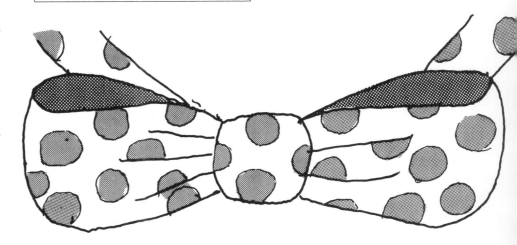

ACTUAL SIZE

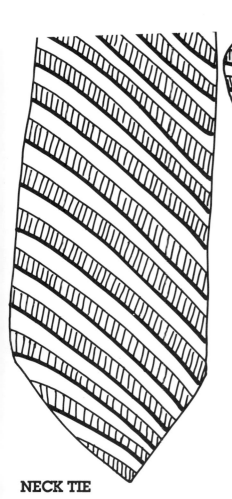

NECK TIE

WHAT YOU'LL NEED

White cotton T-shirt (pre-shrunk)

DMC Floss, a skein of each color:
Red 321, Medium Blue 798, Sky
Blue 800, Rose 758, Gray-Beige
3022

HERE'S HOW:

(Note: use 3 strands thread)

- **Enlarge and transfer** our design
  to T-shirt;

- **work** chain stitch in gray-beige
  around the outline of the tie;

- **embroider** thin diagonal stripes
  of blue and red in chain stitch;

- **fill in** larger sky blue stripes with
  basic satin stitch;

- **work** long and short satin stitch in
  rose in small square of "lining,"
  then outline square in gray-beige
  chain stitch. ■

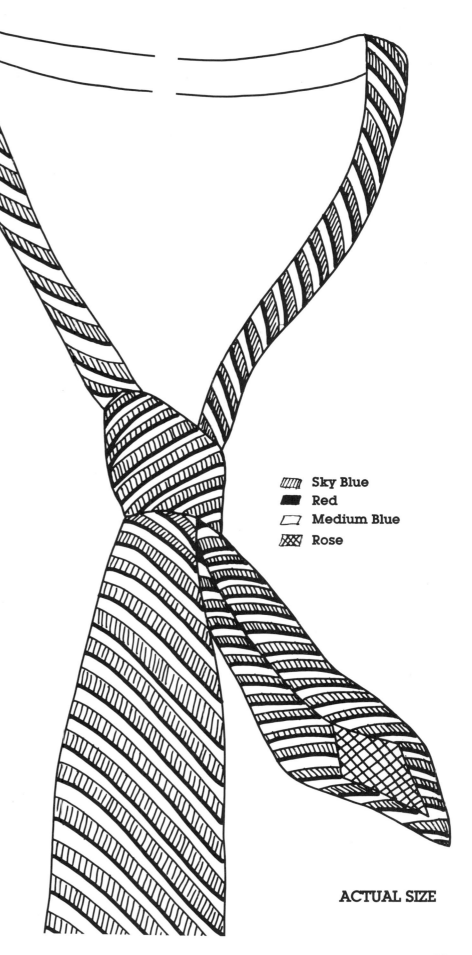

▨ Sky Blue
◼ Red
▭ Medium Blue
▨ Rose

ACTUAL SIZE

BUGS

Yes, the woman on the preceding page does have eight bugs on her sleeve, and yes, they are bigger than life-size. But don't be afraid, they come straight from a textbook and they're embroidered in satin stitch. They are not going anywhere!

When you transfer the insect designs onto your sleeve, insert a piece of cardboard first to make tracing easier. **Photos: pages 82-83.**

WHAT YOU'LL NEED

DMC Floss, 1 skein of each color. The colors are listed along with the names of their bugs.

HERE'S HOW:

- **Transfer** designs to garment;
- **embroider**, using 2 strands thread and satin stitch. (Note: if blouse is pre-sewn, you may have to take out underarm seam in order to place sleeve in hoop.) ■

Anthocomus bipunctus

Exochomus

Meligethes aenus

Thea vigintiduopunctata

Hippodamia

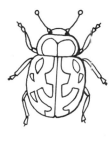

Propylaea

Agonum dorsale

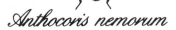

Anthocoris nemorum

ACTUAL SIZE

Anthocomus bipunctatus: Yellows 742 and 727, Greens 991 and 943, and Blue 807; **Exochomus:** Red 666, Black 310, Yellow 727; **Meligethes aenus:** Greens 943, 991, and 704, Yellow 727, Brown 801; **Thea vigintiduopunctata:** Yellow 472, Black 310, Ocre 729; **Hippodamia:** Orange 741, Brown 3371, Red 349, Ocre 729; **Propylaea:** Yellows 726 and 307, Ocre 783, Brown 434, Black 310; **Agonum dorsale:** Red 355, Greens 991 and 943, Brown 301, Ocre 783; **Anthocoris nemorum:** Yellows 783 and 744, Black 310, Brown 976.

TWO FOR THE SHOW

Teen-agers! How many hours does a young socialite spend choosing just the right thing to wear for a big night out? As she tries to decide on a special look for the occasion, she goes through everything in the closet—and then wears what she tried on first!

Help her decide by embroidering a simple dirndl skirt with three happy couples dancing to music of the fifties. Or embroider some nonsensical designs on a tank top and walking shorts. Full-size motifs are provided for all three. **Photo: pages 86-87.**

DIRNDL SKIRT

WHAT YOU'LL NEED

DMC Floss:
For the female dancer, 2 or 3 colors for dress, and a color each for hair and skin; for the male dancer, a color each for hair, skin, pants, shirt, and shoes; for musical notes, use same colors as for dancers.

HERE'S HOW:

- **Transfer** full-size designs to fabric in arrangement of your choice and add musical notes (designs for musical notes are not provided);

Note: if you are working on light-weight fabric, consider placing a lightweight interfacing behind the embroidery for added support.

- **work** notes in stem stitch and fill in dancers with basic satin stitch. ∎

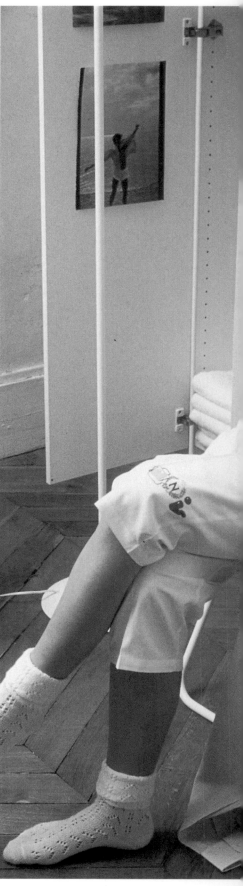

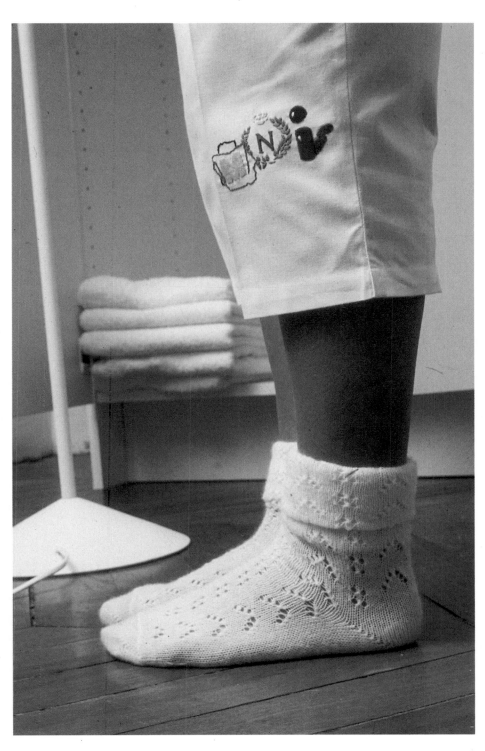

WALKING SHORTS

WHAT YOU'LL NEED

DMC Floss, 1 skein of each color: Yellow 104 (letter "M"), Red 899 (outline around "M"), Black (outline of piece of tape), Blue 792 (letter "N"), Green 702 (laurel wreath), Yellow 726 (imperial crown), Red 817 (letter "i"), Grey 413 (shadow of letter "i")

HERE'S HOW:

- **Transfer** full-size designs to fabric;
- **fill in** large areas with long and short satin stitch;
- **work** outlines in stem stitch;
- **fill in** smaller areas with basic satin stitch. ■

ACTUAL SIZE

TANK TOP

WHAT YOU'LL NEED

DMC Floss, 1 skein of each color: Black (bars, notes, heel and toe of shoes, and shading of "Z"), Green 913 (drinking glass), Pink 603 (drinking straw and glasses frames), Grey 535 (lenses), Blue 995 (shoes), and Yellow 104 (the "Z")

HERE'S HOW:

(Note: Please read about embroidering on stretchy fabrics on page 96 before beginning.)

- **Transfer** design shown actual size here;
- **work** all lines in stem stitch and fill in shaded areas with basic satin stitch;
- **make** "Z" a shadow with stem stitch. ■

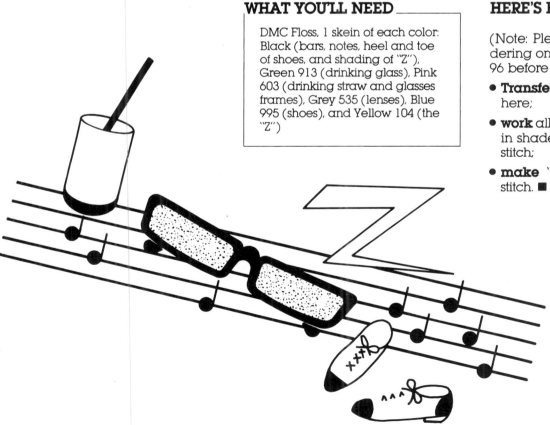

ACTUAL SIZE

INTERPLANETARY EMBROIDERY

Flying saucers, robots, and rockets. They don't make them quite like they used to. If you still hope to come across a little green man someday, be prepared. You can transform an ordinary discount store sweatshirt into a lunar scape or an aerospace base. Embroider an imaginative bit of science fiction.

Our robot was embroidered on etamine first and then appliqued to the shirt, where the lunar countryside awaited him. If you choose to embroider right onto the shirt, be sure the shirt is preshrunk, and that you don't stretch the fabric out of shape as you embroider. For more information about embroidering on stretch fabrics, see page 96.

All three space visitors are embroidered in long and short satin stitch, basic satin stitch, and chain stitch.
Photos: pages 90-91.

FLYING SAUCERS

WHAT YOU'LL NEED

DMC Floss, 1 skein of each color: Silver 762, Blue 995, Yellow 307, Red 666, and Green 700

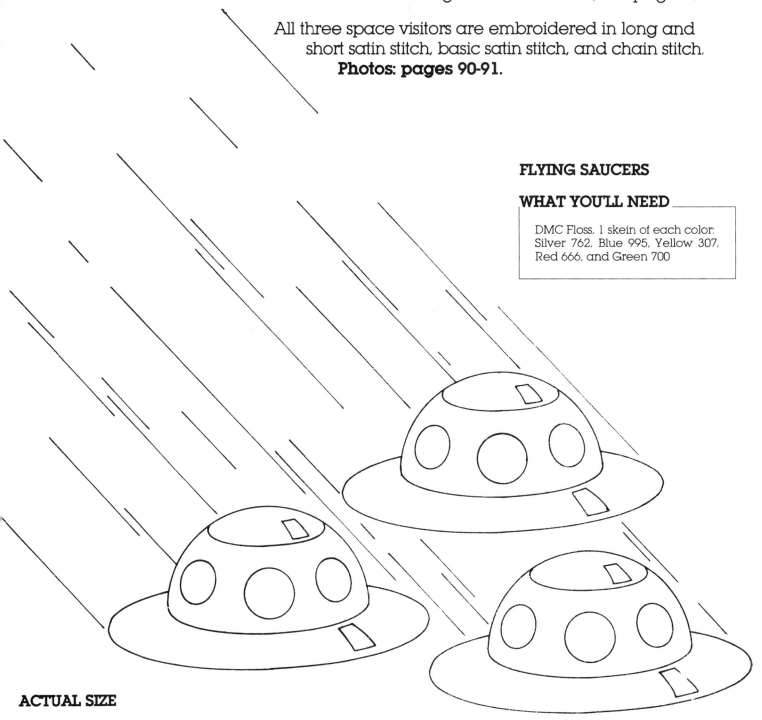

ACTUAL SIZE

INTERPLANETARY EMBROIDERY continued from page 89

THE ROBOT

WHAT YOU'LL NEED

DMC Floss, 1 skein of each color:
White, Blue 995, Light Blue 519,
Yellow 973, Green 704, and Red
666

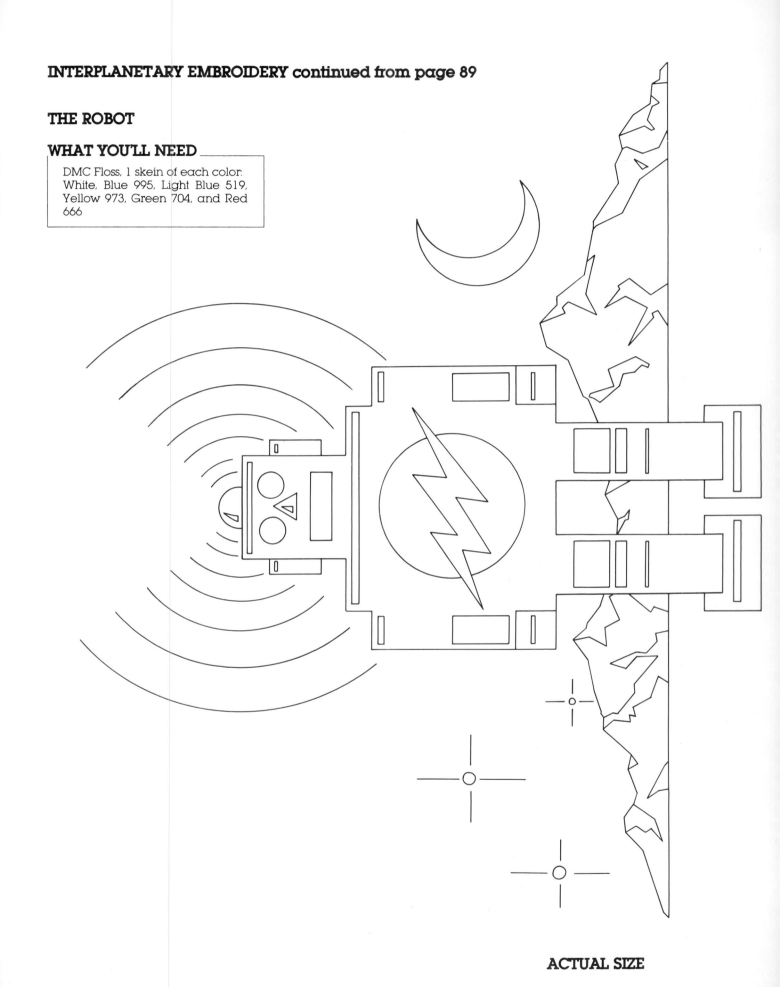

ACTUAL SIZE

ROCKET SHIP

WHAT YOU'LL NEED

DMC Floss, 1 skein of each color:
Red 666, Yellow 973, Blue 995, and
Green 704

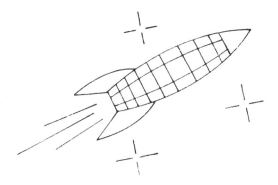

ACTUAL SIZE

THE FAMILY TIES

Many men have a collection of old neckties tucked away in a chest, never to be worn again. And yet, the fabrics are in good condition, and are so beautiful. Put them back to work in a crazy quilt pillow. They shouldn't be hidden away! Best of all, they can provide a fine way to show off your talents with a needle and thread.

To make a 14" (36cm) square pillow like the one shown here, cut two 17" (43cm) muslin squares to be the foundation of the front and back. Select 6 or 7 ties in complimentary colors. Place at least one tie with a pointed end across the pillow front to make the pillow's origin obvious. Pin a tie onto the square and trim off excess. Then arrange and pin the other ties to fill the remaining areas of the pillow front, cutting ties crosswise into thirds, fourths, and so on, overlapping them as necessary. Turn under the uppermost edge and baste the ties to muslin along "seams." Add decorative embroidery along all seams. We suggest using the cretan, fly, feather, blanket, and chain stitch—any or all of them.

Because ties are made of fabric cut on the bias, you can easily make piping from leftover tie fabric if desired. As for the pillow back, it's up to you, you may repeat the front, or make it out of a coordinated fabric. **Photo: next page.**

6 STITCHING ON KNITS

Embroider on a sweatshirt? Of course! On an old sweater? Certainly! It's easy to embroider on stretchy knits if you follow a few simple rules. First, please read "Foundations for Embroidering on Stretchy Fabrics" on page 5.

Always transfer the design to a foundation, rather than directly to the knit fabric. Embroidering on a foundation will help to maintain an even thread tension and will add support for the completed work if you leave a piece of the foundation fabric under the embroidery.

Be very conscious of the tension of your stitches. It should be consistent and not too tight for the article being embroidered; otherwise, the embroidery will distort the knit. You'll need to experiment a little to determine the best tension for your particular project. Try the garment on. Will the area to be embroidered be stretched when the garment is worn? If so, maintain a loose but even tension. The embroidery may not look tight enough when the garment is hanging in the closet, but it will look great when you wear it.

Choose a needle that will not tear the fabric. You will probably need a blunt-tipped tapestry needle for sweaters, and an ordinary crewel needle for lightweight stretch knit fabrics.

When the embroidery is complete, do not press it. Pressing embroidery on knits simply takes the life out of the thread and fabric. They look much better left alone.

PATCHWORK EMBROIDERY

This sweater really is decorated with darning across the front yoke and at the elbows. It has the look of patchwork, a festival of color and geometric designs.

If you have a favorite old crew neck that hides in a dresser drawer because of moth holes or some other misfortune, you can repair the damage and revive the sweater at the same time. Just choose threads and colors that suit the sweater. It's hard to go wrong with this kind of embroidery since just about anything you do will look impressive. Best of all, the embroidery doesn't have to be totally finished before you wear the sweater. You can work on it in stages—it just gets more interesting with each addition.

Basically, this style of embroidery consists of weaving with a needle and thread. First a warp is created of vertical satin stitches or running stitches. Then you weave in and out of the warp with the weft in a plain weave or any weave you like. We offer you some choices here.

A word to the wise: this embroidery is like darning socks. Pull the thread too taut, and you misshape the knit; don't pull tightly enough, and the thread stands away from the sweater. **Photo: page 95.**

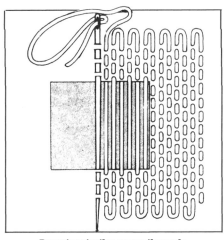

Running in the warp threads

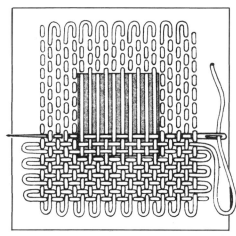

A plain weave—running in the weft threads

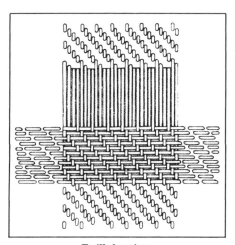

Twill darning

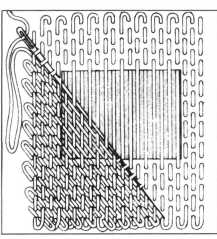

Diagonal darning

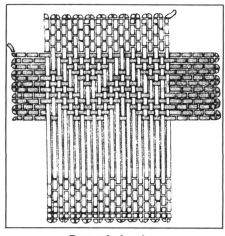

Damask darning

TANK TOP AND LONG JOHNS TAKE FLIGHT

In the men's underwear section of the local department store there is a great variety of knit underwear that can look very feminine when it's dyed and embroidered. Our satin-stitched blue titmouse is inspiring for a young ballet dancer, and the blue-throated warbler draws smiles from whomever this runner passes.

Embroidering on the tank top is a little trickier than on the thermal shirt, because the tank top design will have to stretch with the dancer. Before you begin, read the hints for embroidering on knits on page 96. **Photos: pages 98-99.**

TANK TOP WITH BLUE TITMOUSE

WHAT YOU'LL NEED

8" (20cm) square of waste canvas (very fine)

DMC Floss, 1 skein of each color: Pink 761 (a); Blues 517 (b), 798 (c), 793 (d), 799 (e), 3325 (f), 794 (m), 792 (n); Yellows 307 (g), 492 (h); Greens 368 (i), 320 (j); White (k); Gray 372 (l); Red 817 (o)

HERE'S HOW:

(See page 96 for tips about embroidering on knits.)

Embroider following color key and using basic satin, long and short satin, and straight stitches. Remove canvas when work is complete, a thread at a time. ■

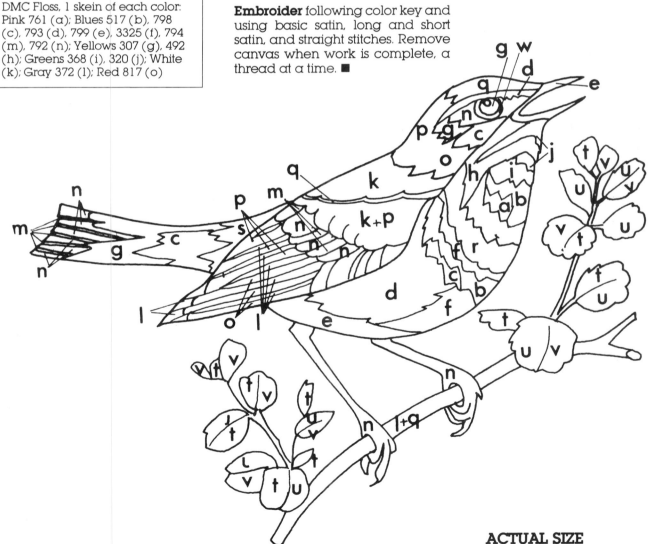

ACTUAL SIZE

THERMAL SHIRT WITH BLUE-THROATED WARBLER

WHAT YOU'LL NEED

8″ (20cm) square waste canvas (very fine)

DMC Floss, 1 skein of each color: Reds 347 (a), 817 (b), 921 (c), 919 (g); Beiges 3033 (d), 3023 (e), 644 (f); Blues 799 (h), 798 (i), 796 (j); Browns 640 (k), 844 (l), 3021 (m), 611 (n), 642 (o), 612 (p), 645 (q), 3371 (r), 3022 (s); Greens 989 (t), 909 (u), 912 (v); White (w)

HERE'S HOW:

Refer to instructions for tank top. ■

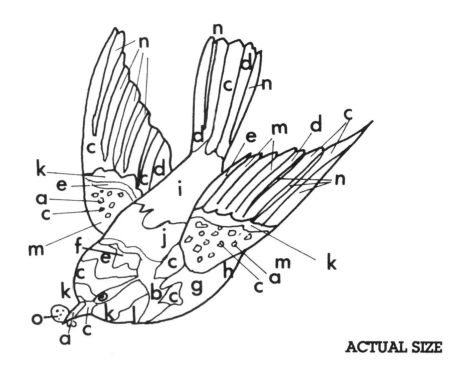

ACTUAL SIZE

A SPRING BOUQUET

A magnificent bouquet of flowers is captured on the back of a simple, lightweight sweater. There are thirty-two colors in all, worked up in satin stitch and stem stitch.

This is a project for the experienced embroiderer. The beautiful, well-executed satin stitches require patience and practice.

Etamine, an even-weave fabric normally used to make pulled thread table linens, is an excellent foundation to use for this embroidery. Read more about etamine on page 5, and read about embroidering on stretchy knits at the beginning of this chapter.

This design would be equally spectacular on a chair back, or framed and hung on a wall. **Photo: page 102.** (Color-coded design on page 104.)

HERE'S HOW:

(See page 96 for tips about embroidery on knits.)

- **Transfer** design to etamine;
- **fill in** with basic satin stitch and outline with stem stitch;
- **remove** etamine thread by thread. ■

A SPRING BOUQUET

WHAT YOU'LL NEED

DMC Floss, 2 skeins of colors 1, 2, 3, 32, 12, and 10; 1 skein of all other colors (numbers in parentheses correspond to numbers on the design): Greens 502 (1), 503 (2), 3347 (3), 3348 (4), 3053 (5), 928 (6), 504 (7), 472 (8); Pinks 554 (9), 818 (10), 819 (11), 776 (12), 3689 (13); Browns 840 (14), 842 (15), 355 (16); Red 321 (21); Blues 334 (22), 794 (23), 798 (24), 800 (25), 827 (26), 931 (27), 932 (28), 909 (29), 996 (30), 995 (31); White (32)

Etamine: 20" (50cm) x 22" (55cm) piece

□ = 2" (5cm)

SWEATERS IN BLOOM

This shetland cardigan (preceding page) displays a bouquet of roses in full bloom right on the shoulder. The more delicate alpaca sweater (page 110) boasts a garden of wildflowers and summer fruits: currants, raspberries, strawberries, and black currants. The fruits and wildflowers trail across the front, back, and sleeves.

In keeping with their textures, we embroidered the shetland cardigan in matte cotton and the alpaca sweater in pearl cotton. The latter's design offers you the chance to use a multitude of stitches: long and short satin stitch, basic satin stitch, French knots, stem stitch, and bullion stitch. **Photos: pages 106, 107, and 110.**

Sometimes embroidering on a light sweater will weight the sweater down and cause the knit to look limp. If that happens to your sweater, sew some lightweight fabric, in a matching color, to the wrong side of the sweater behind the embroidery. Or, use a foundation under the embroidery, but do not remove it after embroidering. Read more about foundations at the beginning of this chapter.

BOUQUET OF ROSES

WHAT YOU'LL NEED

Matte Cotton, 1 skein of each color (the number in parentheses corresponds to the number on the diagram): Gray-greens 2924 (30), 2926 (31), 2928 (32); Pinks 2899 (3), 2776 (2), 2818 (1), 2352 (4), 2921 (5); Muted Greens 2300 (8), 2369 (7), 2715 (6); Tans 2829 (9), 2421 (10), 2673 (11); Reds 2497 (18), 2902 (14), 2815 (15), 2303 (16), 2666 (17); Warm Greens 2470 (12), 2734 (13), 2472 (28); Purples 2315 (19), 2328 (20), 2373 (21); Yellows 2743 (24), 2727 (23), 2745 (22); Blues 2800 (29), 2799 (25), 2798 (26), 2797 (27)

HERE'S HOW:

(Note: Read about embroidering stretchy knits on page 96.)

Work entire design (on page 132) in basic satin stitch (except dotted lines, which are worked in running stitch) following color code on diagram. ■

SUMMER HARVEST

WHAT YOU'LL NEED

DMC Pearl Cotton, 1 skein of each color: Strawberries—3350; Currants—917, 798; Raspberries—962; Cherries—304; Black Currants (blue) 334, 828, (pink) 604, 3687; Corn Poppies—900, 352; Blue Flowers—793, 798; Leaves—703, 503, 3348

HERE'S HOW:

Work design in basic satin and long and short satin stitches, work lines and outlines in stem stitch, use French knots for any dots (tips of pistils in flowers), and bullion stitch for curves on the edges of flower petals, black currants, and center of blue flowers. ■

SUMMER HARVEST

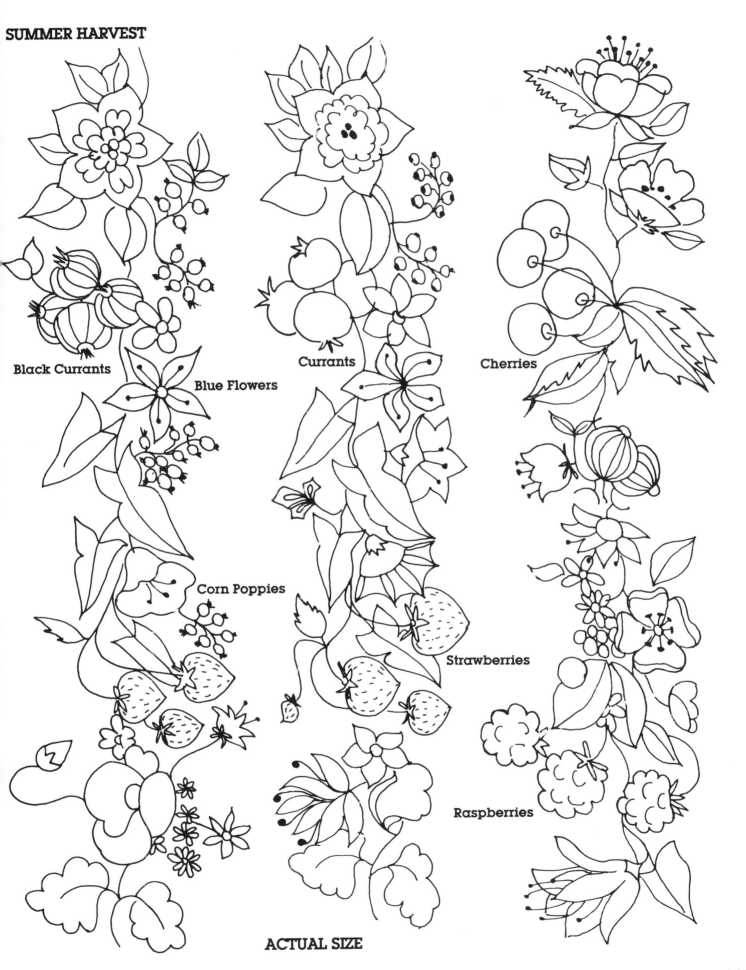

Black Currants

Blue Flowers

Corn Poppies

Currants

Strawberries

Cherries

Raspberries

ACTUAL SIZE

109

7 HOLIDAY MAGIC

The Christmas season provides an embroiderer with plenty of reasons to get busy. It's cold outside, and there are presents to give, entertaining, and lots of special events. It takes all year to get ready.

These pages offer projects for people who like to see little girls in crisp organdy collars, or a parade complete with toy soldiers marching around the center of a tablecloth. There are mistletoe and holly, too. With over thirty motifs to choose from, you should find at least one or two that you can use. And you don't necessarily have to use them as they're shown. The Santa on page 117 would look great on a Christmas stocking hanging by the chimney. The old-fashioned toys could be placed on a double layer of felt and hung at the window or on the tree. And mistletoe embroidered on curtains would be striking all year round.

"NOT A CREATURE WAS STIRRING, NOT EVEN A MOUSE"

For Christmas sentimentalists a very special tablecloth and napkins are a must for the annual occasion. This set is made of inexpensive pillow ticking, and is as practical as it is beautiful. If Uncle Harold spills his wine at Christmas dinner, you'll be able to relax, knowing the stain can be washed away.

Add a friendly mouse among pine cones and berries to each napkin to make your guests feel especially welcome. This gourmet rodent is embroidered in stem, Chinese, and long and short satin stitch. **Photo: preceding page.**

WHAT YOU'LL NEED

Pillow ticking: to fit your table and 16" (40cm) square for each napkin

DMC Floss, 1 skein of each color: Gray 352 (a); Pink 963 (b); White (c); Red 666 (d); Black 310 (e); Yellow 676 (f), 725 (g), 742 (h); Green 991 (i), 992 (j), 993 (k), 503 (l), 966 (m)

HERE'S HOW:

Fill in with vertical long and short satin stitch (menu, berries, mouse and pine cones), work branches in stem stitch, and pine needles, folds in clothing, leaf veins, and letters in Chinese stitch. Use 3 strands of thread. ■

Mouse design for Christmas napkins (photo page 111).

ACTUAL SIZE

TOYS FROM BAVARIA

Bavaria is famous for its celebration of Christmas. Each winter the spirit is rekindled, as every village becomes a child's fantasy of candles, fresh-baked pastries, and bright wooden toys. Bavaria's Christmas spirit is not boisterous, it is quiet, joyful, and utterly traditional.

We can't offer you a taste of Bavaria's delectable chocolate, or the crisp scent of its mountain air, but we're pleased to share some favorite embroidery designs from Bavaria's classic wooden toys. The designs were taken from a toy catalog produced in 1850. The toys' clean lines, their perfect form, and their wonderful colors all helped inspire these delightful embroidery designs.

In keeping with Bavarian tradition, the embroidery is worked completely by hand. Use the designs for a tablecloth and napkins, or place them around the edge of a tree skirt. **Photos: pages 114-115.**

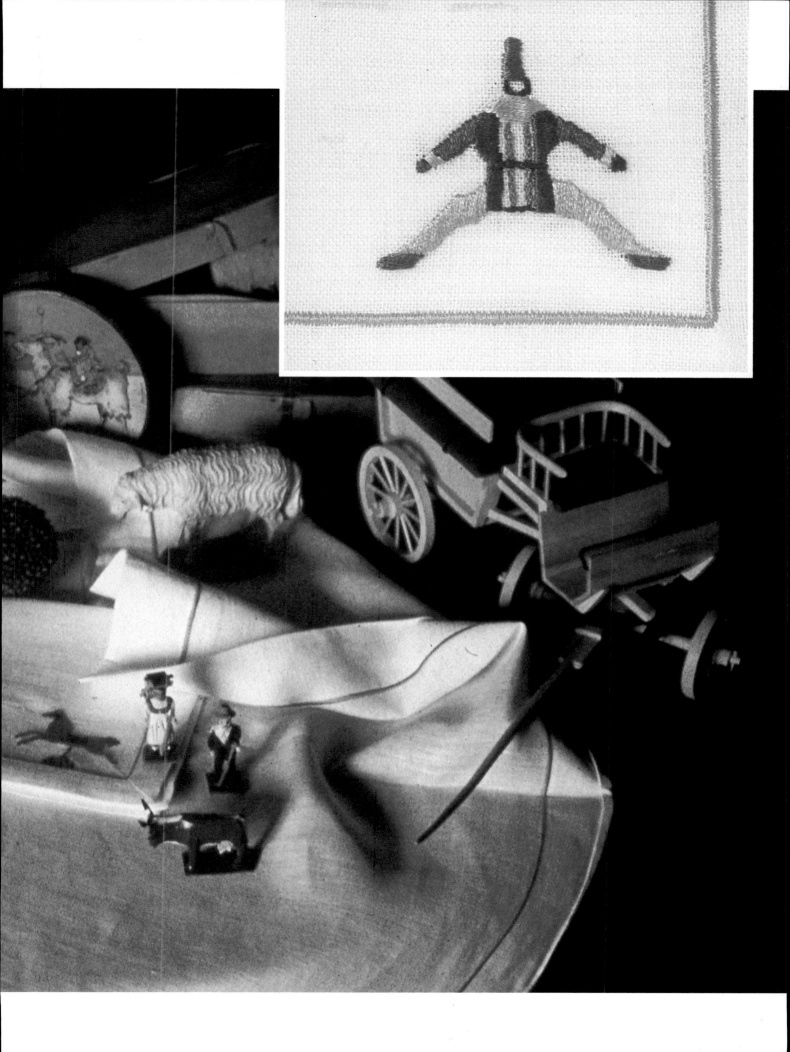

TOYS FROM BAVARIA, continued from page 113

WHAT YOU'LL NEED

Linen, to fit your table and 16"
(40cm) square for each napkin

DMC Floss, 1 skein of each color:
Blues 809, 798, 797; Green 701;
Reddish Brown 919

HERE'S HOW:

- **Transfer** designs to circle at center of tablecloth: find center of tablecloth by folding linen into quarters and pressing creases at center, from center point measure 3½" (8.5cm) to make circle 7" (17cm) in diameter, then scribe second circle 1¼" (3cm) to outside of first circle—use outside circle for a reference when placing tops of designs;

- **fill in** designs with basic satin stitch and long and short satin stitch;

- **outline** with stem stitch and running stitch;

- **cover** inner circle with an overcast stitch (you can use machine satin stitch);

- **embroider** a single motif in corner of each napkin;

- **make** a 2" (5cm) hem around tablecloth and ¾" (2cm) hem around edge of napkins: turn under hem, press, baste, (mitering the corners), and finish with overcast stitch along hem top (or use machine satin stitch). ■

ACTUAL SIZE

"DEAR SANTA ..."

Here's a Christmas list embroidered on a coat, in case Santa Claus needs to be reminded.

A parade of toy designs can give a lift to an old coat that's been forgotten, or make a new one unique. Most of these designs show traditional toys, but you could just as easily personalize with your child's own favorites. If you don't consider yourself an artist, consider transferring drawings from toy packages onto graph paper. **Photos: pages 118-119.**

WHAT YOU'LL NEED

DMC Floss, 1 skein of each color:
White; Grays 415, 317; Black 310;
Red 304; Pinks 603, 948; Blues
823, 518, 747; Greens 991, 993;
Browns 632, 3045; Yellow 727;
metallic silver thread

HERE'S HOW:

- **Transfer** full-size designs;
- **embroider** with 3 strands thread, filling in with basic satin stitch and outlining with stem stitch. ■

White

Silver

Dark Gray

Black

Red

Deep Pink

Pale Pink

Aquamarine

Navy Blue

Light Blue

Dark Green

Light Green

Dark Brown

Light Brown

Yellow

Mixed Colors

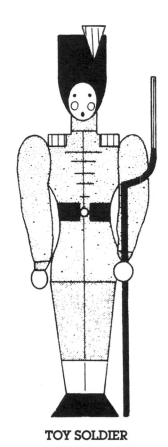

TOY SOLDIER

ACTUAL SIZE

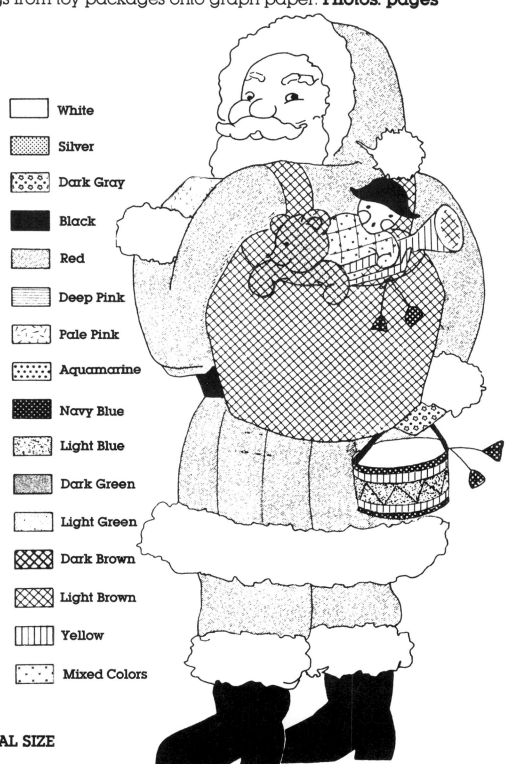

117

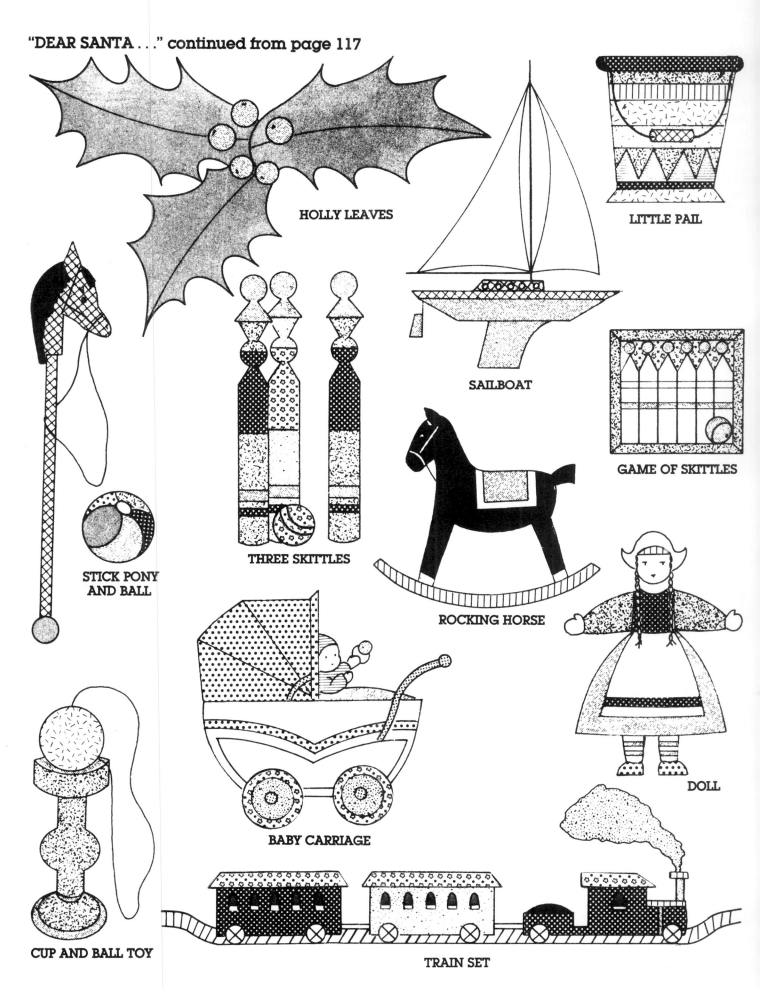

HOLLY LEAVES

LITTLE PAIL

SAILBOAT

GAME OF SKITTLES

STICK PONY AND BALL

THREE SKITTLES

ROCKING HORSE

DOLL

BABY CARRIAGE

CUP AND BALL TOY

TRAIN SET

DRESSED FOR THE OCCASION

Fresh white collars beneath two Sunday faces. Big sister's collar is embroidered with a mistletoe design in pastel colors and edged with a flowing scallop. It's made of cotton organdy. Little sister's is slightly less sophisticated. Pert kittens stand guard around its perimeter while frisky long-tailed mice scamper past. Made of cotton poplin, her collar's shape is reminiscent of the collars of the 17th century.

If the young ladies get their fancy white collars dirty, don't be too upset. These collars are easy to remove for washing. **Photo: next page.**

KITTENS AND MICE COLLAR (Size 3)

WHAT YOU'LL NEED

⅜ yd (30cm) of 36" (90cm) wide white cotton poplin

DMC Floss, 1 skein of each color: 318 (b), 415 (a), 317 (c), Silver (tails and whiskers)

1 small button

HERE'S HOW:

(Note: Collar opens in front.)

- **Trace** pattern and cut according to pattern instructions;

- **transfer** embroidery design to upper collar's right side;

- **embroider** with 3 strands of thread on upper collar only, filling in cats and mice with long and short satin stitch, working whiskers in straight stitch, and mice tails in back stitch;

- **place** upper and lower collars right sides together and stitch all but neck edges;

- **trim** and clip seam and corners, turn, and press;

- **refer** to directions for Scalloped Collar for finishing instructions. ■

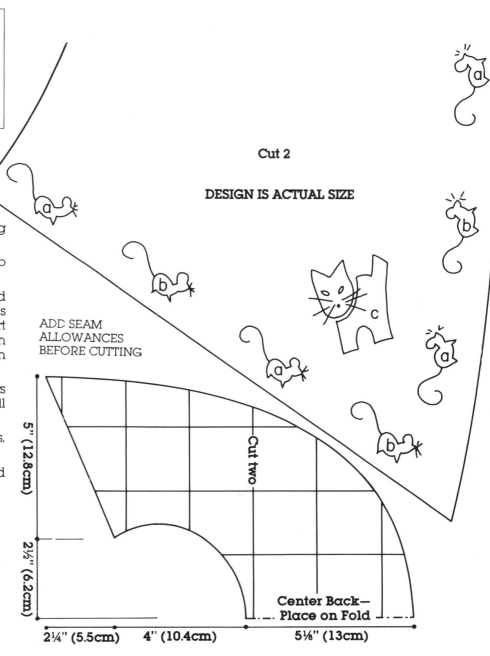

Cut 2

DESIGN IS ACTUAL SIZE

ADD SEAM ALLOWANCES BEFORE CUTTING

5" (12.8cm)

2½" (6.2cm)

Cut two

Center Back— Place on Fold

2¼" (5.5cm) 4" (10.4cm) 5⅛" (13cm)

121

MISTLETOE COLLARS continued from page 121

SCALLOPED COLLAR (Size 5)

WHAT YOU'LL NEED

½ yd (40cm) of 36" (90cm) wide
white cotton organdy

DMC floss, 1 skein of each color:
White (a), Off-White 746 (b),
Mint Green 504 (c)

Brilliant Embroidery and
Cutwork Thread, Size 18: Snow
White (for scalloped edge)

1 small button

ATTACHING BIAS STRIP AND FINISHING

- **Cut** 1⅛" (3cm) wide bias strip the
length of neck edge plus 1"
(2.5cm);
- **stitch** bias strip to neck edge with
right sides together leaving ½"
(1cm) of bias strip free at each
end;
- **press** ends of bias strip to inside
(insert a fabric or elastic thread
loop for button at one end if you
do not plan a thread loop);
- **fold** and press raw edge of bias
strip to inside and slipstitch to
seam;
- **work** thread loop at back neck
and attach button;
- **press** bias band to inside neck. ■

HERE'S HOW:

- **Trace** full-size pattern, adding
seam allowance to all edges;
- **cut** 2 collars as instructed by pattern;
- **baste** upper collar to lower collar
around outer edge with wrong
sides together;
- **transfer** mistletoe and scallop designs to right side of upper collar
as shown on pattern;

- **run** padding stitches along scallop design, then embroider
through both layers in blanket
stitch with Brilliant Embroidery
Thread (see page 24 for detailed
instructions for working scallops);
- **trim away** fabric from scalloped
edge carefully with fine-pointed
scissors;
- **separate** two layers and embroider mistletoe motif, on upper layer
only, with 3 strands thread;
- **backstitch** dotted lines and fill in
with straight stitch.

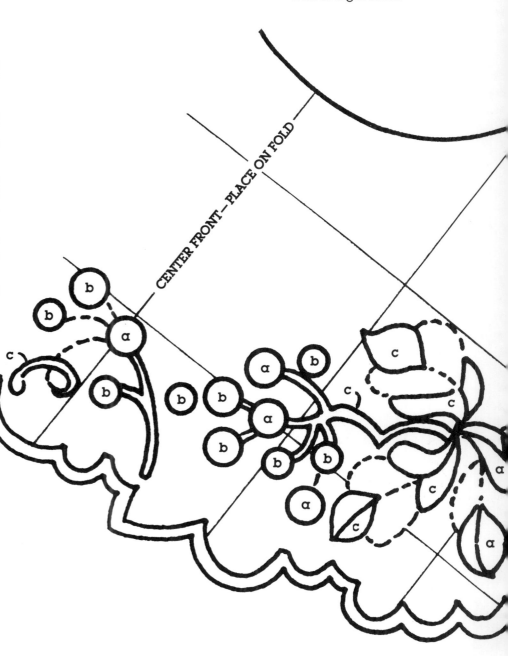

CENTER FRONT – PLACE ON FOLD

124

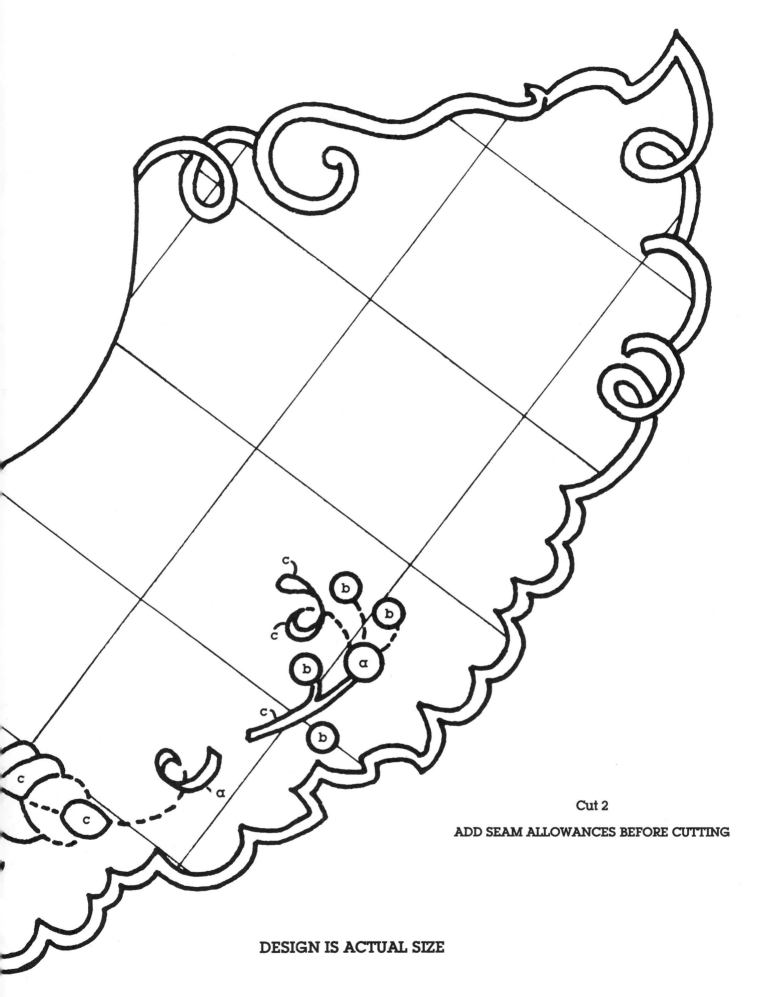

Cut 2

ADD SEAM ALLOWANCES BEFORE CUTTING

DESIGN IS ACTUAL SIZE

QUILTED MISTLETOE

Quilting is the simplest form of free-style embroidery. The humble running stitch connects layers of fabric and padding and at the same time forms berries and leaves of the mistletoe plant. We have used the mistletoe design over and over in window shades, on a velveteen comforter, and at the center of a snuggly bunting. The point is that a simple design can appear elaborate when placed on velvet or accented with fabric paints.

Be sure to keep your fabrics stretched taut while you quilt to ensure a padded look when the quilting is finished. **Photos: pages 126-127 and 130.**

VELVETEEN COMFORTER
(Double bed size)

WHAT YOU'LL NEED

2¼ yds (2.2m) 60″ (1.5m) wide: cotton velveteen and backing fabric

2 pkgs bonded polyester quilt batting, double bed size

8 yds (7.5m) silver piping for trim

Silver quilting thread

Fabric paints (optional)

HERE'S HOW:

- **Transfer** mistletoe motif to center of velveteen in a wreath formation;

- **transfer** a sprig of mistletoe design to each corner of velveteen approximately 6″ (15cm) from edge;

- **paint** design, if desired, according to instructions provided on paints and allow paint to dry thoroughly before continuing;

- **sandwich** backing, batting, and velveteen with wrong sides together;

- **quilt** along outlines of motifs;

- **trim** 1″ (2.5cm) from batting around edges;

- **baste** piping to right side of velveteen, matching edges;

- **turn** all edges to inside and top-stitch close to piping; remove basting stitches. ∎

MISTLETOE DESIGN
ACTUAL SIZE

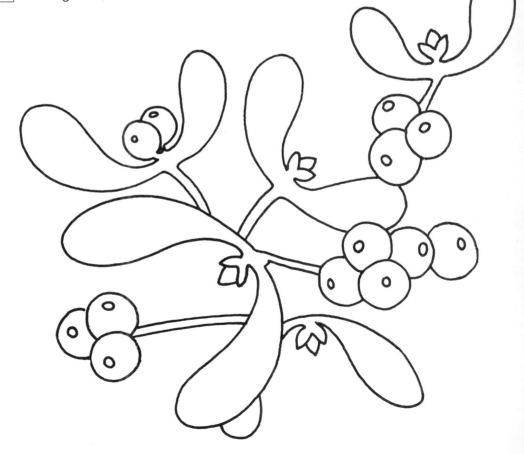

BABY BUNTING (page 130)
Finished bunting is 24" x 28" (61cm x 71cm)

WHAT YOU'LL NEED

¾ yd (70cm) 60" (1.5m) wide:
cotton velveteen and lining
fabric

26" x 60" (66cm x 151cm) piece
quilt batting

Quilting thread

HERE'S HOW:

(Note: Use 1" (2.5cm) seam allowance.)

- **Cut** velveteen and lining to a size
  of 26" x 60" (66cm x 151cm);

- **draw** shell motif on right side velveteen with chalk, using shell template (easily cut from a heavy
  shoebox), leaving space on center front free for mistletoe motif;

- **transfer** mistletoe motif to open
  space;

- **sandwich** lining, batting, and velveteen with wrong sides together
  and baste around edges;

- **quilt** along design lines through
  all thicknesses;

- **fold** quilted bunting in half crosswise with velveteen facing velveteen and stitch "center back
  seam" with velveteen only;

- **match** center front to center back
  and stitch velveteen together at
  bunting bottom, rounding corners;

- **trim** seam allowance from batting, turn edges of lining to inside
  and slipstitch together;

- **turn** top edges of bunting to inside
  and invisibly handstitch top
  closed;

- **turn** bunting velveteen side out. ■

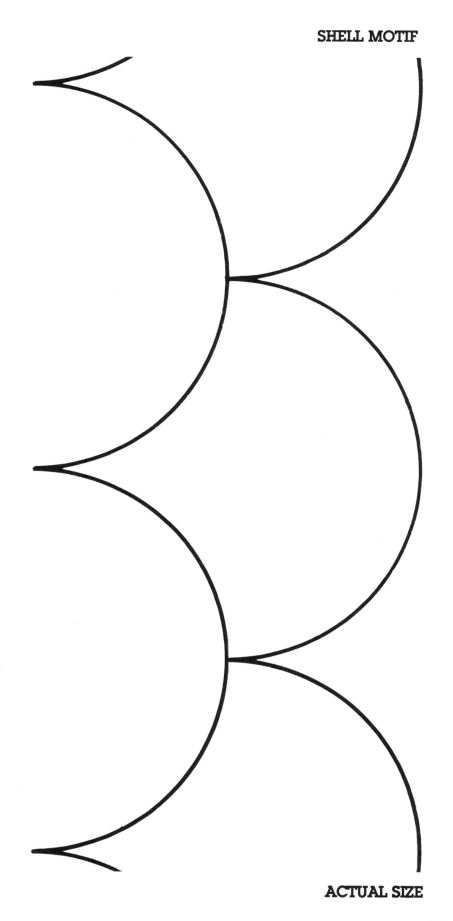

SHELL MOTIF

ACTUAL SIZE

129

Yokes and purse flaps also make attractive showcases for quilting or other forms of embroidery. In each of these examples, a thin layer of batting is placed between the outer fabric and lining to make the quilting stand out. For further emphasis, work with a heavier thread than usual, but do not use six-stranded floss. A quilting thread would perform better through batting. Or, consider dressing up the purse with silver thread as shown here.

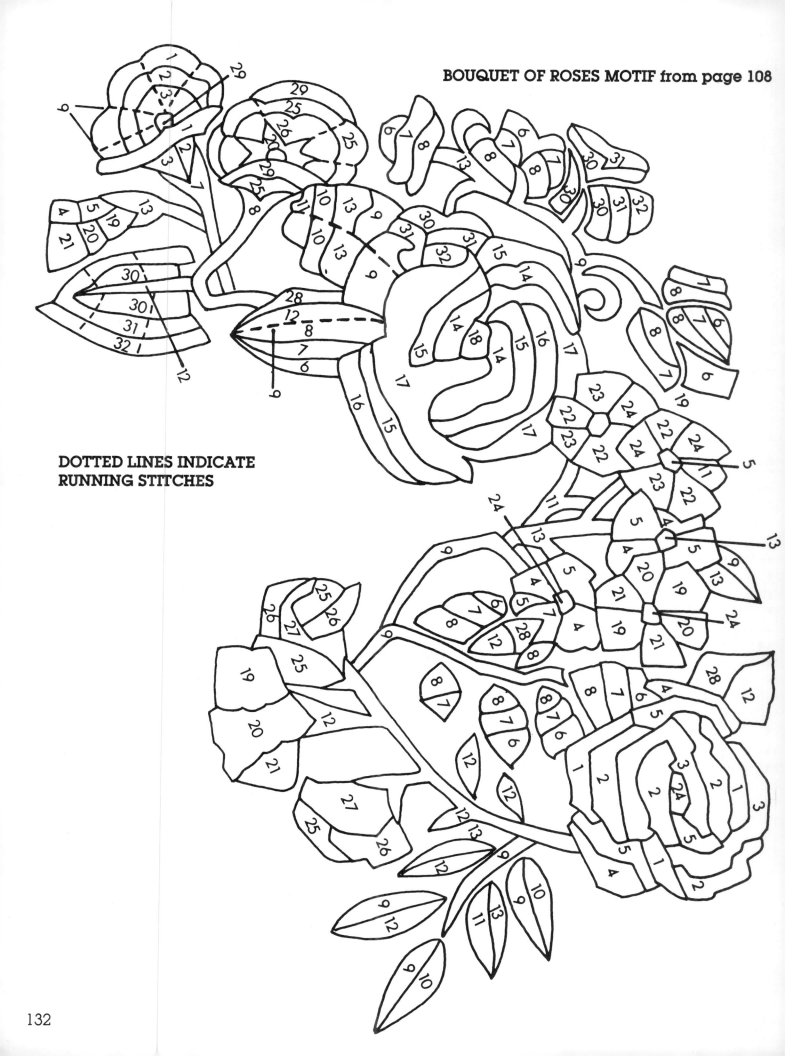

DOTTED LINES INDICATE RUNNING STITCHES

□ = ½″ / 1¼ cm

FOR FURTHER READING

50 Free Style Embroidery Stitches. J and P Coats Limited, 1976, Scotland. A handy pocket size book with clear illustrations and explanations.

de Dillmont, Therese. **The Complete DMC Encyclopedia of Needlework.** Running Press, 1978. Contains 700 pages of information on a variety of embroidery techniques, passed down by experienced embroiderers. Many of its practical tips are difficult to locate elsewhere.

Gostelow, Mary. **The Complete Guide to Needlework Techniques and Materials.** Chartwell Books, Inc., 1982. A very colorful and informative book covering a wide range of embroidery types. Has equal amounts of showcasing and teaching.

Reader's Digest Complete Guide to Needlework. The Reader's Digest Association, Inc., 1979. No book could ever be complete but this one comes very close!

PHOTO CREDITS

The following photographs are from 100 IDEES.

PAGE	PHOTOGRAPHER	STYLIST
Cover, 53	Liddell	Lebeau
25	Duffas	Garcon
28-29	Duffas	Gaudefroy
32-33, 88-89	Maltaverne	Lebeau
36, 76-77, 80-81, 85	Tisne	Garcon
37, 39, 40-41, 56-57	Burgi	Garcon
44-45	Lacombe	Garcon
48-49, 68-69	Duffas	Schoumacher
60-61	Godeaut	Lebeau
72	Godeaut	Faver
73	Tisne, Wincler	
84	Bianchi	
92-93	Bayard	Gaudefroy
96-97	Tisne	Garcon/Luntz
101	Chabaneix	
104-105, 112-113, 116	Chabaneix	Luntz
108-109	Novick	Luntz
117	Maltaverne	Faver
120-121	Bianchi	Schoumacher
128-129	Burgi	Lebeau
132-133, 136, 137	Tisne	Schoumacher

The following photographs are courtesy of HANDMADE magazine.

PAGE	PHOTOGRAPHER	DESIGNER
52	Gillardin	Mimi Shimmin
64-65	Gillardin	Esther Wiberg
100	Brown	Conchita Berry

We would like to thank the DMC Corporation for their help with the artwork in the Stitch Glossary, and Leah Olivier for the alphabet on page 42.

PROJECT INDEX